BECOMING
THE BOSS WIFE

BUILT ON SACRIFICIAL SUFFERING

ISBN -978-1-953788-04-7 **(Printed)**

BECOMING
THE BOSS WIFE

BUILT ON SACRIFICIAL SUFFERING

ANGELA REESE BROOKS

Dedication

This book is dedicated in loving memory to my grandmother, Vernell "Ms. Gin" Walker, for all her words of wisdom. Thank you for giving me the attributes to be a good woman and wife. I love you! I miss you! As promised, I am taking care of my husband.

Acknowledgments

To my husband, Sean, thank you for being my number one supporter while writing this book and understanding that my story had to be told. Words cannot express my gratitude towards you. Our love is much bigger than the world will ever know. I love you!

To my dad, Roy, and my mom, Vermellar, thank you both for instilling principles and values in me. None of your prayers or your hard work was in vain. I love you both.

To my daughters, Seanta', RaSeanda, Seandai, and Zari you girls give me life, and I am so grateful that you all are here to share my Boss Wife journey with me. To my goddaughter Brittany, our talks helped me stay grounded and I am blessed to have you in my life.

To my auntie Tracey "Duchess, who saw my strength when I did not. You are my muse! Thank you for motivating me to be GREAT. There is no other way!

Lastly, to all my good friends, the ones who listened, Andrea, Waltien, Joyce, Zoe and Jon'Elle. This one is special, my good friend, more than a friend, my partner to the end, my sister Jayda thank you for all the conversations, the pep talks, the lunches, and our hugs. You are truly a jewel, and I thank you for encouraging me to write my book.

To the best photographer ever Michael Hawthorne thank you so much for sharing your amazing gift of photography. To my MUA Deanni you are awesome with your brush! What can I say about the best barber in the world other than she is Fabulous "DeetheBarber"(Fadelife4ever) your gift will make room for you!

TABLE OF CONTENTS

INTRODUCTION

Proverbs 31:10(KJV) states, "Who could find such a virtuous woman For her price is far above rubies." No value can be placed on her. Her worth cannot be measured. She is one of a kind, priceless. She is the personification of strength and truth. She is a Boss, Built on Sacrificial Suffering.

I would like to formally introduce you to our guest of honor, "The Boss Wife." When I first envisioned this book, I saw the Boss Wife as the Modern-Day Proverbs 31 Wife. Immediately, I began to describe her characteristics and her beauty in such great detail, but God said to me, "No! that is not it. That is just a small portion of it; it is more than that." God said, "It is massive! It is not a person. It is a process. It is a journey that is orchestrated by Me." Warning: This book will not be for everybody, but I guarantee you it will help somebody. To understand who the Boss Wife is, you must first understand the word boss. The acronym for B.O.S.S. in Boss Wife means Built on Sacrificial Suffering. I am talking to the wife or woman who can relate to this, who has the scars to prove it—the one that has gone through the fire and the storm for her relationship and her marriage. The Boss Wife is for the mature wife or woman who is tired of doing things her way and operating under the spirit of doing business as usual while her marriage is taking a downward spiral. I can testify to that because she is me. My marriage was an absolute mess. My marriage was failing fast! I needed help.

I have been given an assignment from God to deliver a message to the wife, the one who has tried everything in her own strength to save her marriage, only to find that her efforts were unsuccessful. God wants you to move and get out of His way. If not, you are going to mess it up, and He will not allow that, especially when His purpose is attached to the marriage bond. I am living proof of this. God told me to get out of His way concerning my husband, I did not listen, and I did not move. I am sure you can guess what happened next. He forced me out of His way just to get His point across. Let this be a warning when God says move, you better move and move quickly.

God understands the position of marriage right now. He is aware of what you are facing. He knows that marriage is in a state of emergency. He knows that marriage is constantly under attack spiritually. Believe me, the devil will stop at nothing to destroy what God has joined. In this hour, you must be strong as a wife. Spiritual warfare is going to come. You must be ready by putting on the whole armor of God as it states in Ephesians 6:13 (KJV), "Wherefore take unto you the whole armor of God, that ye may be able to withstand in the evil day, and having done all, to stand."
God is not pleased with the behavior of the wife. Too many of you have come into the marriage for the wrong reasons. Yes, I do get it! Your husband may be a good provider, but do not sacrifice your soul or your life chasing after that bag. Remember, you can get your own bag. Some of you are getting caught up wanting the bling, you want the ring, the name, and the fame, but God says not at the price of losing yourself. Do not sell yourself short by settling for just the material satisfaction of the marriage. You are much too precious to God for that. On the other hand, some of you are so weak in your spiritual walk that you will not last two minutes in an actual boxing ring with the devil when it is time to fight for your marriage. Let alone fighting in the spirit realm. Spiritual warfare is real. I would hate to see when that dreadful day comes where adversity hits your home and you have to fight or pray for your marriage. My question to you is, will you grab your sword, which is the Word of God, or will you scramble around to take cover? Some of you are too afraid to be in the trenches and go into battle for your spouse, knowing your marriage is on the line, so why won't you fight? I have been there, did that, and done that, too.

On another note, some of you have been too concerned with what other people think. What other people think concerning your marriage does not matter. But guess what? You are not alone; I was exactly like you.

I let other people's thoughts dictate my actions in my marriage. When you know better, you do better. Now that I know better, I do not live for those people; I live for God. I am only concerned with how God sees my marriage. If God gets the glory from my marriage, then I am good with that. What I have found to be evident and true is that those same people, the ones who are telling you what to do, the ones that are so quick to judge, have real issues just like me and you. They may sit in their glass houses and throw stones at you while pretending that their issues are not real, but believe me, they are dealing with some real issues. Do not be fooled! Everything is not always what it appears to be. I am here to confess that I am a work in progress. My life is real. My marriage is real, and we deal with some real situations. I am not scared to admit that my marriage is a constant work in progress. There is no pretending over here. I know, and I can admit that we need help!

My marriage was FAILING! I knew it, and I could feel it. Take it from me when I tell you that marriage is a serious matter, and spiritual warfare is real. I had a firsthand experience. My marriage was constantly under attack. I cannot make this up, and I will not sugar coat it here. Marriage is no game. It is not a plaything, and it should be treated seriously. If you are not serious, then do not get married. If you are married and you have not been serious, now is the time to get serious. In a nutshell, marriage is for the mature man and woman. It is not something that you just do. Marriage is about longevity. God ordained marriage. From the beginning of time, God joined man and woman together for His purpose. Marriage is all about God's business. God wants the best for our marriages. God wants to see successful marriages. He loves the union of a husband and wife. God wants us to have healthy and happy marriages. I do not know why we act as if we are the ones that are in control when God is the one that created the marriage for His glory and His honor.

For some reason, we have been walking around here as if we control our marriage. We are handling situations according to our emotions and feelings and not how God would want us to handle them. All the while, God is paying close attention to our actions. Remember, He is the only one in control. So, if God is in control, why not go to Him to fix your marriage? Why not seek Him for answers. Why not trust Him concerning you and your husband? You are anointed for God's purpose.

That means you are a big deal to God. Don't you know because of who you are in Christ that God will bless you despite what your husband does? God will get the glory from your life and your marriage.

I am a testimony of what God will do. I was given the assignment to write this book. Because I know that God told me to write these words, I will not downplay anything. Despite what the world may think of me, I will give it to you in the rawest form possible, just as it was given to me by God. I am going to be very transparent in my sharing things with you. Even before writing this book, I can honestly say that I was not ready. I had no desire to give you my testimony or even share my story with you or anybody else in this world. I did not welcome this assignment. I was too embarrassed and too ashamed. I was worried about what they would say. Who are they, you ask? They are the sideline haters. The naysayers. The intruders and the influencers. You know who I'm talking about. I am sure you can relate. You may have come across a few of them in your relationship.

I could not fulfill my destiny because I was too caught up in what would they say if they only knew my truth? So, guess what I did? I hid my truth. I hid my pain. I covered it up. I was carrying the pain around like a concealed weapon. I was locked, loaded, and I most definitely was dangerous. But I was so good at hiding my pain. It was as if I were a chameleon, a master of disguise. I could change my exterior at work to blend with my environment without exposing any of my hurt. How many of us hid our pain so that the world will not see our vulnerability? To be honest, my close friends did not even know that I was in pain. I did not want to be judged again. In the end, who was I fooling? I was not fooling anybody but myself. My truth had to be revealed.

So! God breathes life into this book. This book was birthed out of my internal pain. The pain I did not wish to share with you. I was always taught to keep my business to myself. I was adamant that I was not sharing my pain with anybody. It was too painful. I did not want to be judged. I did not realize that God was already judging me. There was a mandate, an official order by God. God had to birth this baby from my soul. This book came from some hard labor pains. God did a cesarean to get this book out. This book reflects my true self, my personal story. This book is a part of my life. This book is my marriage. This book is all about my B.O.S.S. Wife journey. Everything that is connected to me was Built on Sacrificial Suffering.

As hard as it is for me right now to uncover and expose myself and open the closet door for all my skeletons to fall out about my marriage, I have no other OPTION! I must tell you this because God says I must. I must be so transparent that I help you. You need to know what I have been through to know that you are not alone. Yes! I had to endure some pain, as I am sure you do. I cried many tears, as I am sure you have. I hid it. I buried it. I made it where nobody was aware of it. I experienced hurt and lots of it. I experienced rejection and depression. I even experienced hair loss and weight loss. I lost self-confidence.

I began to question myself and my walk with God. I questioned my life and my purpose. If this story sounds familiar, then you are in the right place. This book is for you. See! I am a testimony. My marriage is a testimony of what God can do and will do. Only God gets the glory. If you are going through something in your relationship or your marriage, please know and understand that restoration can only come from God and God alone. You must have faith in God, not your spouse. God will not make your spouse do anything. Your spouse has a free will to do whatever he chooses, but when there is a purpose attached to you, your marriage, and your spouse, there is a pretty good chance that you will have to experience some growing pains. It could be rocky roads ahead. Do not give up! Gear up! Stick with it! You may have to go through some turbulence for God to get the glory. Sometimes life does send us an unexpected, unwelcoming curveball. Just know that you must go through it, and you are not going through it alone when you have God on your side.

Life at times can send us that curveball UNEXPECTEDLY! Marriage is just like that; sometimes, it can bring an unexpected hit. One that can be so traumatizing that you may not survive. As we embark on this Boss Wife journey together, I want you to travel with me through the most intimate spaces of my marriage. The journey starts with the marriage. You will see how I came into the marriage, not understanding the marriage bond's seriousness. I will take you through my failed attempts to fit my husband's crown. The question is, will it ever fit? As I focused so much on fixing his crown, did I pay any attention to my crown, or did it need adjusting? I need you to travel a little further with me, but I must warn you, BEWARE! Beware of the influencers. The ones you allow knowingly, and the ones you do not know that you allow into your marriage. Now I know that you did not see this coming but come with me as I tell you about the hardest hit, I ever experienced. INFIDELITY! Will I be able to survive? As we move along, you will see that some pain is harder to recover from than others. The question is, will I recover? Will God have to give me a heart transplant to overcome my bitterness and my pain? As we finally come to the end of our journey in the very last chapter, you will find out if there is room for restoration in your marriage.

I pray that this book will be what is necessary to help your marriage, your relationship, your life, and your walk. I hope that it will encourage you to fight for your marriage and give you the desire to work on who you are as a godly woman first and then a wife. God is calling you to make a change. It is time for you to put on your stilettos, grab your Bible and step into your rightful position as "The Boss Wife." May you forever remember this B.O.S.S. Wife's journey, one that was Built on Sacrificial Suffering!

CHAPTER 1

MARRIAGE IS SERIOUS BUSINESS

Marriage is serious business. Marriage is God's business. Some of you have come into the marriage with the thought that the wedding is all there is and what follows is pure happiness and bliss. I am here to tell you that the wedding, as beautiful as it may be, is not all. It is much more. Think about it like this. We will compare marriage as if it were a flower. Just as a flower needs to be nurtured to grow, so does your marriage. It should be nurtured with love, commitment, trust, respect, and honesty. Understand that having a wedding does not mean you have a marriage. A good marriage takes years of dedication and hard work. It is not easy. Believe me, it is not for the weak. You must be strong because there will come a time when your marriage will get tested. It is not a game. Although, many games do get played. It is not something to be played with. Getting married is the easy part. It does not take much energy to go to the altar, recite some vows, exchange rings, and change your last name. The real test is staying married, which can be very hard.

If we were to look at marriage through a Boss Wife's eyes, we would see that it's much more than simply becoming and holding a wife title. Marriage is about loving a person unconditionally despite their faults, loving them even when your marital conditions seem unfavorable, showing someone mercy and compassion when they constantly fail you, and extending grace to someone who may not deserve it. In a nutshell, marriage is a ministry, a God-ordained ministry. It is about the commitment you made at the altar between you, your husband, and God. It is your ministry to your husband.

I know what you might be thinking. If marriage is such a personal ministry, why are there failed marriages involving God-fearing women? It is not that we failed ourselves or that we have failed God. It is a great possibility that we were just not ready for our role as a wife? Maybe it has something to do with our upbringing. Could it be that we vowed not to be like our divorced parents, only to find out that we are just like them? Could it be our current lifestyle? Maybe we are not cut out to be a wife and being single is less stressful than being married (too many rules and stipulations), maybe we tried everything that we could think of to save our marriage only to find out that we married the wrong person what we thought was great potential turned out not to be, or maybe we have attached ourselves to some dream, fantasy, or misconception from our childhood about how a marriage is supposed to be?

With that being said, there are many misconceptions about marriage that I am going to clear up. The first misconception is marriage will change your relationship's current state; this is so far from the truth. If you are having issues now, those issues will not go away. Marriage does not change issues. Marriage sometimes intensifies them. One of the biggest issues out there that can quickly get out of hand is not communicating with your spouse. If you have a communication breakdown before the marriage, that breakdown will still be present. If you have not worked on effectively communicating without cursing, throwing things, having the last word, or merely walking away to avoid engaging, prepare yourself for a life of arguments and misunderstandings. Be mindful that those same misunderstandings can build a wedge between you and your spouse, as small as they appear to be. In some instances, it could lead to him seeking someone who he thinks understands him. Not being able to communicate with your spouse opens the door for many other unwanted issues.

The second misconception is that marriage will change a person. If you are thinking about getting married, be sure it's for the right reasons and that you are not getting married for the sake of ownership (he's my husband now) or that you are trying to prove a point to the world that he loves you. If one of your reasons for getting married is hoping that it will change your spouse, understand that it most likely will not happen until he is ready for it to happen. Forcing unwanted change can be a major problem for your relationship. Understand that just because he married you does not mean his lifestyle will alter or change. Whatever you permitted while dating him, he is still expecting you to agree. If he was hustling, partying, hanging out, and staying out before the marriage, that behavior did not magically disappear because you are his wife now. If you accepted it before, then why not now? If he was overspending, working too much, excessive drinking, smoking, and gambling, these things do not instantly go away. You knew he had a problem with spending; you accepted it then. Just because you have changed does not mean that he has changed. If he has not put away those childish things and made a strong commitment to change, then those hindering, holding back spirits in him could be lying dormant somewhere, just waiting for the right moment to come out. You could avoid the situation and sweep things under the rug, but too much dirt under one rug will eventually resurface. As much as you may want those behaviors to go away, do not count on it. Be prepared that those things only come out through fasting and prayer.

The third misconception is that sex will keep your man. Although sex is welcomed and is a vital part of the marriage bond, connecting sexually in the bedroom is not the keeper when that is the only thing keeping him. Contrary to what some believe, sex is a momentary satisfaction; once that moment is over, it is over. It has no substance. Do not confuse sexual attraction with being compatible as a husband and wife. Marriage is bigger than that. Marriage is, in fact, a spiritual and emotional connection between you and your husband. It is that area of your marriage where your husband knows that he can trust you with his life. That you will constantly pray for him even when he is wrong and that you will always have his best interest at heart.

The fourth misconception is that he (your husband) makes you complete. We hear it all the time from women "girl, he completes me." So, does this mean that getting married would make you whole? Were you not all put together before marrying him? Houston! We do have a problem. No one should be completing you other than God. Don't you realize that this idea of someone else making you whole places limitations on who you are? You do not want to give anyone this kind of power. Know and understand that you complete you and God completes you. God is the only one that has this kind of power.

Lastly, the fifth misconception is that marriage will solve the problem of being lonely. With that loneliness comes unhappiness. Who wants to go through life being alone? For this reason, we go out and find someone we believe we can build and grow with. Sometimes we do not have to be looking for them; they find us. In essence, we then marry someone we believe will make us happy, and we no longer will endure being lonely. But what happens when we find out that the person cannot make us happy and he fails. It is not that we have chosen the wrong person, but maybe our expectations of that person were unrealistic. True happiness does not come from an individual, money, or things; it comes from God. In marriage, you will find that you may still be lonely, you may still be insecure, and may still be unhappy. Marriage is not always going to make you happy, but it will make you better.

Every misconception that I spoke about I had. I walked into a marriage with unrealistic goals for my husband and me. I felt he completed me. When God completed me! I believed that once I married him, he was exclusively mine. But he had not put away his childish behavior. I tried to change him for the better. He resisted because he felt a woman could not tell him what to do. I gave him as much sex as possible, but it did not matter. He was selfish. Our relationship did not change because we were married. God knew from the very beginning that we would have all sorts of issues, and we have had all sorts of issues, but he joined us together anyway. It was more like God allowed the union to take place. Never be so quick to judge if you do not know the purpose.

Most people would not have lasted as long as I have. Some have even said to me, "girl, you are crazy. I would have been gone," I am here, not in my strength. All I can tell you is that when God has a purpose and you are attached to that purpose, the very thing that everyone thought would FAIL, the very thing that everyone wished would fail (you know what I am talking about) like your marriage. God can come in and make a 180-degree difference and change everything instantaneously. God will use your marriage so that He would get the glory. That is what God is doing in my marriage. God will shock the ones sitting on the sideline, hoping, and waiting on its demise.

From the very beginning, our marriage was a test for this testimony. When I committed, I mean a serious commitment to God and surrendered all, God did a miracle in me. God infused his presence in me as a wife. Believe me, I take my marriage seriously, and I war in the spirit for it daily. Now my husband, on the other hand, is weak in some areas. It is true that he has made a lot of mistakes in this marriage but so have I. Some of you reading this have made some mistakes too, so who are we to judge? The one thing that I do know is that God knows my husband's heart. I do not worry about what the world thinks. What the world does not see is when my husband prays for me. My husband prayed for God to save our marriage when I refused to. When I had given up totally, he asked God to heal me. I am a witness that God does change somethings. It may not happen overnight; in my case, it took 22 years, to be exact. It took 22 years of our marriage for my husband to put away childish behavior. Understand that we do not operate on our timing but God's timing. My husband is a work in progress. God is still working on him but in God's timing. Although, we have suffered many things. We are still married and working at getting better, not for the world but God.

My true romantics believe in the fairy tale marriage involving prince charming and living happily ever after. Sounds perfect, right? Understand, however, as much as we strive for perfection, there is no perfect marriage. Why? Because perfection implies flawlessness.

Newsflash! Your marriage will not be perfect. Some things will be perfected, but they will never be perfect. Admittedly, there are couples out here winning in their marriage. They are doing it big, they have great communication, and they are successful. Note that this did not happen overnight, and the result that you see did not come without pain. What you may be witnessing is the aftereffect of the storm that they could have faced. Be prepared to experience turbulence in your marriage. Some turbulence may cause you to view your spouse differently. Marriage deals directly with our imperfections. All of our flaws are exposed because we are not perfect; we are all works in progress. Marriage is hard work. Marriage will not do the work for you. You will have to work at it. I hate to break it to you now, but it is time for you to erase the happily ever after syndrome from your mind. True happiness will come from God, and your marriage should be centered around God. God should be the foundation, and we should be following His divine plan for our marriage. From the beginning of time, God had a divine plan in place for your marriage. We can see this in Genesis 2:24 (KJV).

"Therefore, shall a man leave his father and his mother and shall cleave unto his wife, and they shall be one flesh."

Marriage was designed to be a life-long covenant between a husband, a wife, and God. A covenant filled with commitment, companionship, and fruitfulness. The marriage reflects the Trinity. If the marriage is not taken seriously, the very image of God will be tarnished. The reason marriage is so serious is that it is supposed to mirror God's love. But somewhere along the way, we have missed the mark. Staying married is no longer an option and has now turned into a momentary contractual agreement that can be broken at any time. What was once Holy, the institution of the marriage is not sacred anymore.

Sacredness of the Marriage

We are living in an age where marriage has become commercialized and materialistic. Social media is our go-to for everything, and it is dominating our daily lives. It is so easy for us to get caught up trying to keep up with the Joneses. We are practically emulating their lives. We have fallen for the hype. While we are pretending, our marriages are failing. The frivolous things of this world have taken precedence over the sacredness of the marriage ceremony.

The marriage ceremony, which was once an intimate moment to share with our friends and family, has now turned into a competition. More emphasis is being placed on the material things associated with the wedding and less on the spiritual. We want to have the most exquisite wedding ceremony, one that is filled with over-the-top centerpieces, designer dresses, and gorgeous stationery. Simultaneously, the sacredness of the marriage bond has been forfeited for a fairytale wedding experience. Who are we trying to impress here? The people or God?

We are spending more time and money on planning and preparing for the wedding and less time building the marriage. We are so caught up in setting the next trend that we bypass the most important part, which is God. The bride-to-be has become more concerned with the beating of her face instead of glowing spiritually in God's grace. From the wedding attire to the order of the ceremony, down to the proper etiquette requirements for the way guests bring gifts, every detail is being considered, but not once have we considered including God. God is no longer an option or a guest, and because of this behavior, God is not pleased. We have become blinded by the pomp and circumstance of the wedding and cannot see God's plan for the marriage. We move further and further away from God, and now the wedding ceremony has become an idol. Marriage has become a mere accomplishment, not a commitment. It is just another trophy to sit on the shelf. The sacredness of the wedding ceremony has been forgotten. We have ignored God's purpose for the marriage. To be very honest with you, the state of marriage is in trouble.

State of the Marriage

Too many marriages are failing. The state of marriage appears to be in turmoil. The term marriage is now being associated with the term overrated. Being a godly wife is looked upon by some as being unnecessary. Meaning that there is no value placed on being married or being a wife, let alone a godly wife.

Why? Could it be because of their carnal operations? Could it be that the wife is taking a worldly approach to a spiritual situation? This is so easy to do. Often, we try to handle our issues and problems ourselves. Instead of seeking God for answers, we are turning to ungodly counsel and ungodly behavior. For example, some godly wives are being counseled by their single girlfriends, not that there is anything wrong with that, but being a godly wife, you must be mindful of who you confide in and what you tell them. Word to the wise: Do not go around telling your intimate secrets to people who cannot keep a secret. Seek counsel that will hold you accountable to your vows, your husband, and God.

Beware that many marriages have ended because of outside influencers. You have a responsibility as a godly wife to guard your marriage with your whole heart. Another reason the state of the marriage is in trouble is that it is better to be single than married. Some feel it is okay to shack up and live together with no strings attached. Why get married when being married does not seem any different than being single.

In some cases, wives are stepping out on their husbands and husbands stepping out on their wives. It does not make sense; no one is committed. No one seems to be faithful. The question is, why even think about marriage? When you have so many examples around you that are failing. Christian marriages should be the epitome of all marriages, should be setting the tone for how the marriage is supposed to operate according to God's plan. However, those same Christian marriages are failing at an all-time high. They are failing even faster than ungodly marriages. They are failing because they are human and not perfect. You must begin to look at marriage the way God looks at marriage. You will see that marriage is good. God ordained the marriage for His glory.

The Marriage Journey

Marriage is not about you. Just remove yourself from the equation. Marriage is all for God's glory. It is all for His purpose. Marriage is about loving unconditionally. It is about giving your all when you do not want to. Marriage is about sacrificing. Sometimes that is the hardest thing to do. I had to learn this the hard way. There is no I in team; marriage is about teamwork. What I did not understand at the time was that it was not all about me. In marriage, there is no room for individuality but unity. When you are married, you and your spouse should operate as one union. When I first got married, I had no clue about what I was doing. And I had no idea as to how to be a wife. All I knew is that I was married. It is so easy to have the wedding, to wear his ring, carry his last name, and have no earthly idea how to be his wife.

There was no handbook or guide to show you what to do. Life will be your biggest teacher. When I got married, I did not know how to be a wife, not to mention a godly wife. So you mean I have to be mindful of the things I say and the things I do? Even when he offends me? I did not know how to love my husband, satisfy him or, pray for him. I know what you are saying. Didn't you guys get counseling before getting married? Well, sure, we did. Getting counseling does not prepare you for marriage, especially when you are not ready. Before getting married, we had counseling sessions with my pastor, but he did not give us the real deal. I believe he sugar-coated it a little not to scare us. But I wish he would have scared the hell out of us for us to make a strong and wise decision about getting married. He did not give us what we needed to know. He did not tell us that one day we may experience pain from one another, we would struggle in our finances (because my money is mine and his money is his), that we would experience adultery that would almost kill our marriage, experience betrayal from each others not to mention from family members, and that one day we would get hurt by our closest friends. He did not tell us that we might wake up and realize that we are sleeping with the enemy. We were not prepared mentally, and honestly, we messed up.

Every marriage has its challenges, but problems came in like a whirlwind for us in our marriage. I will not say that we were unequally yoked; I believe that we both love God. But I will say that we were off-balance. Something did not click. Our goals did not align. What I do believe is that our biggest challenge was becoming one flesh and making decisions as one. How could we when we both were too stubborn to communicate, and communication was our greatest downfall? We operated separately. We did things separately. Besides having the same physical address, we lived separately, sometimes in different states. I was okay with him being gone and he was okay with not be alone. We operated as individuals, not as a married couple.

In our marriage, we struggled with commitment, respect, and honesty. If I can be truthful with myself looking back, neither of us was prepared for the marriage, and our age had nothing to do with it. Maturity had everything to do with it. We were not mature. Being married is certainly for mature folks. I hate to admit it, as much as I wanted to believe that my husband wanted to marry me, really loved me, I knew deep in my heart he was not ready to be my husband, somewhere in the back of my mind, I thought I was ready to be a wife. Oh boy! Was I wrong? I wasn't ready at all. I thought I had chosen a king, but he was not ready to wear a crown. As much as I wanted it to fit, his crown did not fit, and I knew it. That did not matter to me because I wanted so badly to make it fit. How many of you know that the man was not ready for you as much as you were ready for him? He was not ready to be a king. You knew it, you felt it, but you wanted it so much. You wanted to prove to the world that he was ready to be your king. Only to find out that he could not be a king or a jester because he was not ready.

Be Patient! Change Will Come

I share my story with you in hopes that it will help you along the way. Marriage is a rough journey and I am not there yet. I have not arrived at my destination. I am still traveling on my Boss Wife journey; believe me, every day is different. For our marriage, every day is a God-filled day. Slowly, our marriage is changing, and there is some hope. If you are going through something in your marriage and you feel that there is no possible way that your marriage can recover, let me reassure you that God can change the impossible. When the world says it is not possible, God says it is.

God can change your heart and the heart of your husband too. God can breathe life into the dead areas of your marriage. He can change your situation for the better. Believe me, I have been there. You are not alone. A year ago, I was there, and my marriage was over because I said enough, and it was over. But there is hope because there is God. Let me give you a little bit of advice. If you want to see a change in your marriage, go back to your first love, which is God. Reestablish that relationship. That relationship is more important than any other relationship in this world. Once you align yourself with God, everything will work according to His will, not yours. Invite God into your life, marriage, and home and see what the result will be.

Maybe you were like me; you just got into the marriage, never giving it a second thought; you did not fully surrender it because you still needed to be in control. You thought that you could change your spouse and even your marriage. Only to find out that you are powerless. God is the only one that can make any kind of change. Restoring, rebuilding that is what God does. He loves marriage. He ordained it, so why not restore it? Know and understand that God is the only one that can bring restoration to your marriage.

Yes, marriage is important, but self-love means everything. If you have not done this, I want you to love yourself; love yourself enough to know your value and know your worth. Understand who you are, "Boss Wife." Do not just accept anything because you love a person. You are worth much more than that. I want you to love you more; when you can love you more, you can give your marriage so much more. Physically, mentally, and spiritually.

Last, love your spouse as God loves your spouse. We all have flaws. Nobody on this earth is perfect. Once you have done all of this, I want you to pray for your marriage and ask God to cover and restore it and to give you a new love, new zeal, and a new marriage. Ask God to build it the way that He wants it built. Consult and hear from God concerning your marriage. No more talking. Listen for God's voice. After this, if you are serious about saving your marriage and you are sure that God has told you that this is the man that can wear the crown as your king, then, and only then do you fight. Fight in the spirit realm, grab your sword, which is the word of God, fight with all of your might for your marriage. Just as in the game of chess, you will need to step into your position as the Queen. What the Queen does on the chessboard is most powerful; her ultimate and only goal is to protect her King. Time out for playing. It is time for you to get into your position as a wife and protect your king because marriage is a serious business.

LESSON 1- MARRIAGE IS SERIOUS
1. After reading this chapter, do you think that you have taken your marriage seriously? If not, what can you do to get things right?
2. Have you, for any reason, forfeited the sacredness of the marriage bond?
3. Take a good look at the state of your marriage right now today. Is there anything that you would want to fix?
4. I want you to close your eyes and think about your marriage, your husband, and your walk as a wife. Have you been behaving like a wife or a knife? If you have what can you do now to change your behavior. Have you consulted God for the answers?
5. Do you want a healthy and happy marriage? Are you willing to give it all you got, or will you give up and give in?

CHAPTER 2

HIS CROWN DOES NOT FIT

His Crown

Today, we call the man our king without knowing if he has the full potential to wear the crown. The term is being used loosely without understanding what is required to be a king. It is no wonder his crown is not fitting when we are prematurely crowning him by giving him this title. He is not earning the title; we are forcing it upon him. We push and push for the man to be everything we envision him to be as our king, not realizing that the man we chose may not be fit to be a king or a jester (fool). But we are calling him our king. We require his behavior to reflect a king when he was never taught how to be a king. How can we expect his crown to fit when he does not know how to honor you like a queen?

For the sake of this text, we will be referring to the crown as the man's spiritual walk. This walk is reflective of who he is as a man first, then a husband. The crown shows off the man's true position as a husband, revealing the truth of who he is. Good or bad. The crown signifies the husband's attributes the ones he should possess as a godly man, such as being loyal, faithful, committed, a leader, independent and spiritual. His crown is not physical. It is spiritual.

If his crown is not fitting, that is a red flag, an indication that something may be out of sync or just plain out of order. Sometimes this may also mean that the man may not yet be in a position to receive you the Queen as his wife. On the other hand, it could simply mean that the man is just not the right one for you. Remember, Queen, when selecting or choosing a man (king) you want to spend the rest of your life with, you must thoroughly examine his crown. Warning comes before destruction. Pay close attention to the warning signs because they are there for a reason. Please do an extensive examination of his crown before marrying him because his crown may not befitting.

I Did Not Wait for God

I did not wait on God to prepare my husband. I also did not seek counsel from God before marrying him. I married my husband because he was my friend, we connected so well, we understood one another, and I loved him. Not to mention he was the father of my children, and it felt right, like the right thing to do. Looking back at the beginning of our relationship, I did not consider my husband's attributes when examining his crown. Quite frankly, I believe that I did not examine his crown at all. To be honest, if I had, he probably would not be my husband today.

Now I am sure some of you can relate to being so caught up in the illusion of love that you can admit that it is so easy to lose sight of what is important to you. What is important is the fitting of the husband's crown. During this period, my husband's crown did not fit. Honestly, it never did quite fit because he did not want it to fit. I always tried to fit it on him. Here is some food for thought: you cannot change someone that does not want to change. I attempted to use force to get his crown on him, a crown that I envisioned him wearing, instead of allowing God to crown him in the spirit of excellence as a godly husband. I did not give my husband time to develop. I intercepted God's plan. I took matters into my own hands. As soon as I put my hands on it, I messed it up. For some reason, I always thought I had to do things my way as if God needed my help.

A few words of advice: Do not get married just because the man is your child's father, do not let your feelings or emotions be the controlling factor of your decision either, and do not allow people to shame you into marriage. There are plenty of people who did not get married just because they had a baby. Take into consideration everything and be sure to examine his crown thoroughly. The man you choose must be able to wear the crown as your king. His crown must fit. There is no room for negotiating here. You two must be equally yoked. There are marriages out there right now that probably should not be because of being unequally yoked.

Consider his crown. Your union must be right in God's eyes. I am speaking from first-hand experience. I never one-time asked God questions that normally might have been a deal-breaker for me. I operated out of sheer emotion. All I knew was I loved him, and I wanted to be his wife. Do not confuse lust with love. I should have stopped, pumped my brakes, and asked God key questions like was this the man He chose for me, is this man a good provider, can I depend on him to carry me when I fall, is this man someone that can lead and I follow, is this man connected to God spiritually that he can pray for me when I am weak and does this man possess the qualities of a godly husband?

Remember, I said at the beginning of this chapter that I had to do it my way. Well! I did. I took it upon myself to crown my king. I could have waited for God; I should have waited for God. But sometimes, we tend to think that God takes too long, not realizing there is a reason behind His delay. What I have found to be evident and true is that God will not stop us from our desires. The heart wants what the heart wants, and my heart wanted to be with my husband. God did not stop me from doing what my heart desired. God will give us our hearts' desires even if there is a lesson of pain attached to it.

Crown of Loyalty

1 Corinthians 13:11(KJV) states, "When I was a child I spake as a child, I understood as a child, I thought as a child: but when I became a man, I put away childish things." Because my husband said I do, I was under the impression he had put away those childish things. I assumed he was ready to be my king, so I thought the crown of loyalty would have been an easy fit for him when I tried placing it on his head. Instead, he resisted in the spirit realm by slapping it away. The crown of Loyalty was supposed to be his transformation from a boy into a man. No longer operating from a single man's mentality, free and independent from that lifestyle. I assumed that he would be loyal to our marriage and me now that I was his wife. I was met with resistance because he was not READY.

Although he was a man, he was not mature enough spiritually to receive or appreciate me as his wife.

Crown of Leadership

Ephesians 5:23(KJV) states, "For the husband is the head of the wife even as Christ is the head of the church and he is the savior of the body." I thought maybe if I adjusted the crown of my husband just a little, the crown of leadership would surely fit. But I am sure you can guess that the crown of leadership did not fit. Through my eyes, I saw my husband as a leader. I wanted him to take on the role and responsibility as the head. Maybe that was too much responsibility for a man that was not ready to be a husband or a king. God later revealed to me that my husband lacked leadership. To lead, you must know how to follow, and he was not yet following God. So how could I expect him to lead as my husband? God said to me:

> "I do not care how well put together you may think he is; he is not ready. He was not given the tools to be successful in marriage. He still has a lot of learning to do. Just because he is a man does not mean he has reached maturation. You have been observing the wrong thing. You see his outer man, which is good-looking, but I see his inner man, and it is broken. He is not READY.
>
> For him to lead, he must first know how to follow me. I gave him examples for him to follow, and those examples failed. He looked up to his father as any young boy would, and because his father did not know how to love, he instilled the wrong values. His father displayed a life of infidelity and unfaithfulness, and he failed. He worked, he also provided, but he was a hustler. He failed the little boy that looked up to him. In turn, he turned to the pastor, and because the pastor was an abusive husband, he too failed. None of these examples of men showed him how to follow; they failed. Where they should have been instilling the things necessary for his success, they all failed to show him how to be a good man, how to love a woman, how to lead by example, how to be a provider, and how to be a godly husband." They failed! He was not prepared, and believe me, he was not ready!"

As much as I wanted my husband to lead, I can admit that I was not fully ready to follow because I was so independent. The leadership role did not mean he was telling me what to do, but it was him stepping into his rightful place as the head, the visionary, the husband that God made him be. I had to learn that my resistance was hindering his growth. God made me take a back seat.

God said, "If he fails, he fails, but at least for once, he tried, not you. Now you get out of his way."

Crown of Spirituality

Placing this crown on his head is easy. Surely the crown of spirituality would fit. He grew up in the church, and I know he knows God. But in his spirit, man, I had no idea that there was warfare taking place. I did not know he wrestled with somethings internally. It was as if he had no peace, no love, or gentleness. I realized that this was because he had not yet surrendered all to God. As his wife, I wanted more for him spiritually. I did not want to see my husband go to Hell. I wanted his deliverance so much that I neglected my spiritual self. Do not get me wrong, I did not throw the bible at him. I did not force the bible either I just wanted us to grow spiritually together. How many of you know that this can be a problem?

Well, I wanted all these things, but that is not what he wanted. He was not ready spiritually to give up the world. I knew he had a love for God. There was no question about that, but he was deep in the world. Sometimes when you can be so wrapped up in the world that you become the world, he was not lame to the things of the world. He was knee-deep in it. He was not squeaky clean either. But there is one thing I know about God: God will not tolerate this lukewarm behavior. My husband's lifestyle was unhealthy for me spiritually and not pleasing to God at all, and I knew this. I tried hard to change him.

Listen to me, you cannot change a man's heart. The heart wants what it wants. Numerous attempts were made to change him, and I FAILED! Now, didn't I tell y'all that God told me to get out of the way a long time ago? Once again, I did not listen. How hardheaded could I have been? Have you ever heard the saying that "Warning comes before destruction"? Well, that statement is so true. The Holy Spirit gave me a warning. The Holy Spirit told me that "I needed to get myself together, and if not, God was going to do it for me." Not only that, the Holy Spirit revealed to me that I was hindering my husband's spiritual growth. It was made clear that my husband's spiritual walk was his own walk, not mine, and that I needed to stop trying to change him. Guess what God did? He removed him. God removed him for a season. Sometimes a couple of seasons. God removed him for me and for God's purpose. God had to sit him down to slow him down. God gave him time to think. If it takes incarceration to change, convert, and correct your spouse. God will not require any approval from you to do so. God will do what He says because God is who He is, and in the end, God will get His point across, especially when there is a purpose attached to it.

Thinking back, I remember this one moment of sitting in the courtroom. I had a million emotions running simultaneously, not knowing what the outcome was going to be. If you never experienced this situation, the entire process can be nerve-racking. I was nervous for him. Constantly having to talk to this lawyer and the next lawyer, I felt like a criminal. As much as we would like these moments in time to pass by quickly, God allowed this one moment to linger. This is one time I recalled myself just pleading with God to step in. I said, "You are in control, Lord. Just deliver him," but God did not because God had a plan. God's plan was not my plan. God did what He said He was going to do. Yes! You guessed it. God removed him. That very day my husband did not walk out of the courtroom a free man. It was not the system that failed him; it was his choice that got him there, but God locked him up.

I was hurt because I wanted him home, but I was embarrassed by the outcome. Because of that embarrassment and shame, I could not ask anyone for help. Sometimes, when your spouse cannot quite get it together, people tend to look at you differently. I started thinking about what the church, my friends, and my family would think about me now that his crown is EXPOSED. His true self, his lifestyle is now revealed to the world.

Here is a word of advice you better stop worrying about what they think and worry about what God thinks. The incarceration period was necessary for my husband to draw him nearer to God. Change can only come through God, and sometimes it takes drastic measures like incarceration to bring about real change. Jumping in and out of the street life can cause a man to choose which God he really wants to serve. Proverbs 3:5-6(KJV) states, "Trust in the Lord with all your heart, and do not lean on your own understanding. In all your ways acknowledge Him, and He will make straight your paths." The world may not understand, but God does. God had to make straight my husband's path, not man. No matter how long it takes for him to see the vision that God has for his life.

Crown of Vision

"A man without a vision is a man without a future. A man without a future will always return to his past" (P.K. Bernard). I wanted a future for my husband. I did not want my husband to return to his former life, his past, so I was constantly praying for God to give him a different vision, a new outlook on life. Everything has its own timing with God, and it was not time yet. I knew that for my husband to wear the crown of Vision, he would have to be so tapped into the vision that God has for his life that vision would supersede his thought process and expectations.

I knew that once he was tapped in, then and only then would he finally get it. He would be open to receive the vision God has for our marriage. He would be able to see our marriage through the lenses of God, separating his own connection with the things of the world. Now he would be able to see me as his wife, his blessing. At that time, he could not see.

Because I saw more for my husband's life and wanted more for our marriage, and I knew his having sight without vision was detrimental to our marriage, I tried hard to fit the crown of vision on his head. I promise you I was met with so much resistance. The things that I saw, he could not see. His vision had not yet evolved. His 20/20 vision needed to be adjusted, so I tried to help him along the way. His vision was blurry. Often when a man's vision is blurred, he cannot see beyond his current state. He could not see with godly vision because he was not ready. He operated by his sight. He had no idea where God wanted to take him. He could not see the plans that God had for his marriage because he was blinded by the lust of the world. A man that has no vision has no purpose.

LESSON 2- HIS CROWN DOESN'T FIT

1. Is there something about your husband that you wish you could change? Are you guilty of trying to fit his crown?

2. In what areas do you feel that your husband struggles the most? Have you consulted God about this issue? If you have not, then stop and ask God to deliver your husband.

3. Write down seven times what you would like God to change in your husband. Because 7 is completion with God, we will believe that this exercise will be the end of all that is wrong. Then I want you to go to Psalms 91. Read it completely first, and then write Psalms 91 over what you have just written about your husband. Write it so that it covers the words entirely. This is you believing that God has covered your words. Fold the paper up and put it away. God's hand will move.

CHAPTER 3

ADJUSTING MY CROWN

The Crown of the Queen

As a Queen (wife), you have a great responsibility that has been placed upon you as a wife, and that is always to protect your king(husband) as if you were in an intense game of chess. The crown that you wear is your strength. It is the power you hold as Queen (a wife). You are his Queen. You are a part of a royal lineage in Christ Jesus. You are a godly wife ordained by God himself. You are a B.O.S.S. Wife. You have a legitimate right to wear the crown as Queen (his wife). Let us look at what Proverbs 12 says about you.

She is the Crown of her Husband

Proverbs 12:4 (KJV) states that "a virtuous woman is a crown to her husband: but she that maketh ashamed is as rottenness in his bones." According to this scripture, the wife is considered the crown of her husband. In all its embellishments and splendor, the crown is intended to adorn the head of the king (her husband). She makes him look and feel good. The wife's crown is the King's (husband's) Glory. As delicate as she may appear in the natural, the wife is not inferior by any means; she enhances and strengthens his character as king. She helps him to be a better man. Her crown is amazingly beautiful. Not only does she contribute honor, respect, and dignity to her husband, but she compliments his fly (style), his swag, and his image. He is proud that she is his crown, his wife, and his Queen. He praises her to everyone. It is an honor that she is his wife.

But what happens if the wife's crown is not intact? What if the wife's crown does not compliment her husband's character and the crown she wears has made him ashamed? We know that the crown is a representation of her spiritual walk. But what if her spiritual walk is not pleasing unto God? If her walk, her speech, and thoughts about her marriage do not line up with what the word of God says, the result could be detrimental to her husband and her marriage. Just as the word of God says, this behavior could cause rottenness (sickness) in his bones, in his spirit, and his soul, for she is the wife that he had chosen.

If the wife is not operating as a godly wife, maybe she is not ready. She could have come into the marriage under a pretense. She thought she wanted a husband, later realized that she only wanted the provision that could come from being married, like the house, the car, the clothes, and the bills being paid. She did not take into consideration what would be required of her as a wife. It is too much. She is not ready to be a wife, not to mention a godly wife. She loves living her single life with no strings attached. Although she is married, she operates as if she has no husband. Her behavior is not honoring or pleasing her husband, and her crown is now stained. Her stained crown is a bad reflection of how the world perceives her king. Surely if he is not honored and respected by his own house, how can the world respect him? Remember that a good wife makes her husband look good, but a bad wife is like a cancer eating up and consuming his body, leaving him hollow like an empty shell. The question is, which wife are you? Are you being considered as a blessing to your husband, or are you a curse?

A Blessing or a Curse

I must admit that I did not operate as a blessing to my husband early in my marriage. As much as I would have like to put on the façade that I behaved like a prim and proper Queen, that would be so far from the truth. Honestly, sometimes there was nothing royal about my behavior or my speech. My crown needed adjusting. I am the first to admit that I operated as a curse in my marriage or at least the words that came from my lips did. Proverbs 18:21 (KJV) states that "Death and life are in the power of the tongue." You must be mindful of what you say and how you say it. Every single time I cursed my husband, I was cursing myself.

My behavior was not a good reflection of a godly wife, and my character was far from pleasing God. I did not act a fool in public, but I did many times lose it. My crown was supposed to reflect my walk as a godly wife, but my behavior caused my crown to be tainted. To be honest, my crown and my spiritual walk needed a lot of work. I was and still am a work in progress.

Back then, I was not blessing my husband with my words. I was causing death spiritually. My words cut deep enough to wound his soul. I functioned as a knife, not a wife. I did not build him up. I used my words as weapons of mass destruction to break down my marriage, to break down my spouse. Clearly, my husband was no angel, and he probably deserved everything I gave and then some, but God was looking at me. God was looking at my actions. My actions were only reactions because I was hurting and experiencing pain. I wanted to hurt my husband the way he was hurting me. The same pain he inflicted in me, I wanted to give it back to him in return. I could not physically do it, so I did it with my words. Honestly, my crown was damaged, and because I did not fully understand what it meant to wear the crown of a godly wife, I failed.

Understanding Your Crown

To better understand what the crown represents to the wife, we must first take a deeper look and examine it. To the natural eye, we see the crown in its physical state. It is more than physical it is spiritual. The crown portrays the spiritual walk of a woman. A woman that is on a mission to be a godly wife. This woman is not perfect. Her crown is stained because of life. It displays all the things we as women try so hard to hide; all the imperfections we try to hold in or escape from are so elegantly displayed on our crown.

As much as we do not want it to be, our true self is EXPOSED! We make attempts to disguise our hurt and pain from the world. But you cannot miss the crown because you wear it upon your head. There is a saying that first impressions are a lasting impression. Your crown is the first thing that people will encounter. If your crown is not fitting, it will unveil you. All the things you try to evade, all the pain, all the emotions will be out in the open, and it is REVEALED! Guess where? On our crown, of course.

The world may not know who you are under your crown because you have been able to conceal your identity behind all the Mac makeup, the contacts, the weave, the breast, and butt implants, but God does. You can run, but you cannot hide your true self from God. God is omnipotent. He is an all-knowing and all-seeing God. God knows your heart. He knows your walk. God knows your pain. God deals with the heart, and He knows the issues of your heart. If nobody knows the real you, God knows the REAL you, and God sees your crown.

The jewels and gems in your crown are just the attributes you as the wife should possess, and those same attributes should be a great contribution to your husband and your marriage. But for some reason lately, your crown is tainted. It appears that you have lost something. You have noticed that your walk as a wife has become stagnant. You are no longer evolving in the marriage. The crown should display the fruit of the Spirit, which is love, joy, peace, longsuffering, gentleness, goodness, faith, meekness, and temperance. Your crown is the opposite. Your desire for marriage is not the same.

It appears that your crown has another plan. One that you think is hidden, but it is not. You could be hiding it from the world, but God sees it. When things get rough in marriage, it does weigh heavy on the crown. Just understand that grass is not always greener on the other side. You may be moving according to the way you feel and not God's way. God is not pleased. You have been operating in your flesh and not the Spirit. This is a sure indication that your crown needs to be adjusted.

If you do not believe me, take a step back, look at your walk, and look at your crown. Examine who you are in God, and then, and only then will you understand the reason behind wearing your crown. If the crown is important to you, I am sure you will agree that it is time for your crown to be adjusted.

Here is a golden nugget after examining your crown: just ask yourself if your crown, your walk, talk, and life are pleasing to God. If your crown is not pleasing unto God, then there is no way possible that your crown can please your husband. If you truly want your marriage to work, it is time to fix your crown. Stop pretending you are not perfect, and yes, you will mess up; I sure did. But now it is time to step into who you are as a Boss Wife and get this thing right once and for all.

No Pretending

No more pretending. Let us be honest. There is no perfect wife. Stop trying to be perfect! Stop trying to put on for the world. Get real and try to be the best wife that you can be. God is not looking for you to be perfect. But God is always looking! God wants you to be the wife that He designed you to be.

We often change our faces and identities a hundred times before becoming the godly woman God intended us to be. I can say that I have had multiple identities or personalities. Not that I am crazy or anything, but I often reacted in my flesh. I can honestly say that I have since graduated from the days of throwing ashtrays, swinging crowbars, flattening tires all 4 of them (y'all know this takes a long time), and even pulling out a pistol, and if it was not for one person's interception, I could have changed the course of my own life forever. Thank God for change. Thank God for changing me.

My walk was not perfect. There were so many times that I tried hard to perfect my walk. But my emotions constantly got in the way. I tried, but I did not let God do it for me. See, I was a good wife. I did all the things that I felt a good wife should do, but I was not perfect. I am human. I was not perfect, neither was my walk. I pretended that I had it all together. That is because I was too afraid to be honest with myself. I was not ready to be a godly wife or a wife. I thought I was ready. But mentally, I was not wifey material according to God's word, but to the world I was. I was hardworking, dedicated, and faithful. What man would not want that in a wife, right? But I still had a carnal mindset. It was not anything spiritual. Even though I had a spiritual foundation, my mindset operated on how marriage worked in the world, not in the spirit realm.

God was yet calling me to go deeper, but I was not cooperating. I still operated in my flesh. I did things how I wanted to do things. I handled situations in my marriage how I wanted to handle those situations, and it was nothing godly about the results. I did not always pray for my husband;

sometimes, I could not stand to be in the same room with him. Believe it or not, I was going to church, and I was studying my word, but I was not living as the word says that I should live as a godly wife. I am not talking about disrespect from disrespecting myself as a woman or my body. I am talking about the words that came from my lips about my husband, about our marriage.

When my husband offended me, I wanted some get back. As much as he would give it to me, I gave it right back. Neither one of us would back down. We struggled hard in this area. I was a foolish wife. Proverbs 9:13 (KJV) states that "A foolish woman is clamorous; she is simple and knoweth nothing." For the foolish wife or woman operates in destruction. She lives for the get back. She destroys and ruins her family, home, marriage, and legacy by her own decisions. She does not seek the counsel of the Lord, for the world counsels her. That is what I was doing. I was destroying my marriage. I was not sowing life into my marriage; I was killing it.

Be mindful of your speech and what you put into the atmosphere. Those same negative words can grow and become your reality. Take it from me, I have seen it happen. There was so much hell that broke loose in my house that God had no other recourse but to step in. Thank God for stepping in. Thank God for giving me a desire to want to be a godly wife. Change was so necessary. If I could have seen my spiritual crown during that time, I am sure that it was hanging on by a thin thread; it needed adjusting and replacing. That is how bad it was, and God knew it. My behavior was not pleasing before God. There was no question that there would be rocky roads ahead of us because of my actions. I did not know what I was doing at the time, but I had been plucking my marriage down with my own hands.

A Wise Woman Buildeth Her House

Proverbs: 14:1 (KJV) states, "Every wise woman buildeth her house: but the foolish plucketh it down with her hands. Keep in mind being a woman in a marriage does not make you a wife, it does not make you a godly wife, and it doesn't make you a wise wife. Anyone can wear the title of a wife, but what does it mean to be a wise wife? A wise woman or wife desires to improve the state of her marriage, her family, her home, and she builds legacies. She builds her house. She builds her house on a foundation that goes beyond a physical and sexual attraction to her husband. This wise woman's house is built on the word of God. She uses her knowledge and wisdom to empower her household. She sacrifices everything for her family. She is the modern-day Proverbs 31 woman. Proverbs 31:11 (KJV) states that "The heart of her husband doth safeth trust in her, so that he shall have no need of spoil." She is resourceful. She does not operate unwisely about her husband and her marriage. She looks out for the best interest of her husband and family. She is a godly wife with great responsibility.

Becoming A Godly Wife

Becoming a godly wife comes with great responsibility. This is something that I have been expressing from the very beginning that marriage is serious business. It should not be taken lightly. Being a godly wife is more serious than anything. It is so serious that God himself took a piece of the man, put him in a deep sleep, and made a woman. This is how precious you are. God designed you to be your husband's helpmate. Adjusting your crown means that you will do what is necessary to become a godly wife despite how you feel in your flesh.

Think back to the day, the moment, the second, and the hour when you recited those vows for better or for worse, in sickness and in health, until death do us apart. Those were not just words spoken with empty promises. You made a commitment as a wife, not just to your husband but to God. Now it is up to you to honor your commitment and fight hard for your marriage.

Let us talk a moment about being a godly wife. What does it entail? First, let us look at what exactly does it mean to be godly? Godly means having the characteristics of God. Not that you are trying to emulate God, but you want your attributes to mirror His character. You want to be pleasing before God. To get a better picture or a better understanding of what it truly means to be a godly wife, let us look at Proverbs 31. This chapter of Proverbs gives us a pretty good idea of what type of wife pleases the Lord. The wife that I am speaking of has God's heart. She fears the Lord. She is not afraid to have the Holy Spirit work through her. She is a worshipper and a believer. She is being transformed daily into a new creation. A godly wife is consumed with the fruit of the spirit, which is love, joy, peace, patience, kindness, goodness, faithfulness, gentleness, and self-control. She is growing into a mature, godly wife. She knows how to handle herself and her marriage God's way. She knows that when her husband offends her, she must behave like a godly wife and pray for him.

The Behavior of a Godly Wife

Proverbs 18:22 (KJV) states, "Whoso findeth a wife findeth a good thing, and obaineth favour of the Lord." You are a good thing, and you should be treated as such. Every marriage has its ups and downs but know your worth. When your husband offends you, I want you to pray for him. Never lose the lady that is inside of you by reacting like a man. Behaving in a tit-for-tat situation will not work in a marriage. Proverbs 14:1(KJV) states that "Every wise woman buildeth her house but the foolish plucketh it down with her hands." So be mindful of the actions you take.

Marriage is serious business. Do not play with it. You will live a life of regret in the end. Some marriages have ended in divorce prematurely because they did not consult God and operated from a worldly perspective. These marriages have failed. They moved when God did not tell them to move. Now they are left emotionally shattered and scarred. It is time to get real and to make a change. Because the marriage is in trouble, God is calling you as the wife to get into your rightful position. Order must come back to the marriage. It depends on you. The sacredness of the marriage must be redeemed. It is time for a serious-minded commitment. You need to get serious about your spouse and be serious about God. There is significance in your role as a godly wife. Your marriage depends on you. If the marriage does not operate properly, then the image of God is marred. If your marriage is not reflecting the image of God, then you must make some serious changes. Those changes must come from within. You must come to grips with the reality of who you are and who God wants you to become as a godly wife. You have a serious assignment, and your marriage depends on it.

Coming To Grips

We all have those moments in our lives where we must come to grips with the harsh reality of who we are and who we have become. All the things that we were ever told about ourselves, whether true or false, no longer hold any weight. At this very instance, we must take a good look at the woman in the mirror and be completely honest with ourselves. As much as we may adore or hate the features of the woman in the mirror, we have reached a breaking point in our lives where we have to dig deeper and examine the soul. There we will find all her flaws, imperfections, and all the insecurities that she has, and we take ownership of them. The woman in the mirror is a mere reflection of yourself; it is us looking back at ourselves, and in our observation, we notice that there is still something missing. Something is out of place, and we get an eerie feeling that something is just not right. Suddenly, it hits us like a boulder falling from the sky, and we have a profound epiphany. Reality sets in, and our truth is now realized. Then and only then can we finally admit that we are not perfect. We are only human, and our crown needs adjusting.

The World Does Not Define Me

For some reason, when we think about adjusting our crowns, we tend to look for the world to validate us. We have given the world the authority to be the defining factor of who we are and who we are to become. I know most of us will not admit this, but the truth of the matter is that we all have. For so long, the world has told us how we should look, how we should dress, how we should speak, how we should act. We have been told what we should drive and where we should live. It is funny how society and people can have you second-guessing your own identity. I can admit that for so long, I had been seeking validation from people without realizing it. I recall being very young, maybe in grade school. I did not look like all the other little girls. They all had straight, pretty teeth, and it felt like I was the only one with a space or gap between my teeth. I could not understand it at that time. I wanted those other little girls to accept me and validate who I was. As a child, I was not there yet. But I know that God made me different for a reason. He had a purpose for my life. That same space between my teeth was an eye-catcher, but what proceeded from my lips would be a soul grabber.

Adjusting my crown dealt with all my imperfections. See, the validation that I was seeking comes from God Himself. My husband nor anyone else on this earth can validate me, only God. God is the only one that defines me and gives me my identity and my purpose. Adjusting my crown is about adjusting me. It is about me realizing who and whose I am. It is about my essence and my soul. It is about me finding and accepting my true self. It is about me knowing my value and understanding my worth, and no matter what the world says about me, they cannot define me. No longer is the world, and the people in it, allowed to be my voice. My crown represents who I am in God and who I am as a godly wife.

My Crown Represents Who I Am

The crown represents who I am in God, not who I am to this world. My crown is my spiritual walk. It is my spiritual connection to my creator. According to the word of God, I am more than a conqueror. That means that I am stronger, wiser, and that I can endure in any battle. Romans 8:37(KJV) states, "Nay, in all these things, we are more than conquerors through him that loves us." When reading this scripture, I get it now, and I understand and know who I am. I stand on the fact that God loves me, and because God loves me, I can overcome adversity in my life and my marriage. Adjusting my crown meant no more limits or limitations in my life and my marriage.

According to Philippians 4:13(KJV), "I can do all things through Christ which strengthen me." I understand that I can do all things not in my strength but with God. When everything else around me was failing all, I had was God. It is true my crown needed adjusting, and God was the only one that could do it. The crown represents my relationship with God. It is Him dealing with my internal self. It is about me taking ownership of who I am. It is about me stepping into my destiny and my purpose. It is me walking and talking in the way that God wants me to. It is about me being who God made me to be – a godly wife. I am walking in my destiny and operating in the calling that has been placed on my life. My crown may be tilted. It may be withered, and it may be worn, but it has weathered many storms and survived. My crown is still intact. Everything I am is because of who God predestined me to be. I am a wife. I am a godly wife. I am the Boss Wife, Built on Sacrificial Suffering.

Adjusting My Crown

Adjusting my crown is about understanding who I am as a woman first and as a wife second. To get to this point of realizing who I am, I had to do a lot of self-examining. This process helped me understand that adjusting my crown is all about me stepping into what I was predestined to do. It is about me walking into my destiny and my purpose. Adjusting my crown is my relationship with God and how I handle and carry myself as a woman and a wife. It is about my character, dignity, and self-respect, and it is about honoring my Father in heaven. Adjusting my crown has not always been an easy task because I am human, and I have human emotions that drive my thought process. I have real situations, pressures, and real-life issues that I deal with daily. I am in this world, but I am not of this world. Adjusting our crowns removes us from the world's way of doing things, and it switches gears to doing things the way the Lord wants it done. Adjusting my crown is about dealing with who I am. It is about me surrendering all and giving it all to God, never one time looking back at my past. It is about forgiving myself for all my past mistakes and all my regrets. It is about trusting me and trusting God. It is about loving me. I want to love me more than I ever loved a man.

Every day that I wake up is a day that God preordained for me to operate in my purpose. My marriage is an example of me walking in that purpose. My marriage was not easy. God had to heal me internally before I could be a blessing to my husband. Because of life, my crown was tainted, and I lost my identity. I had been concentrating and focusing so hard on fitting my husband's crown that I neglected my own. Sometimes God has a way of reaching us. At times He may do it with a little nudge or a push to say, "Hey, I am trying to get your attention," but there are other times when He will use drastic measures, painful encounters, and maybe death of a loved one to get our attention. I think I have experienced a little bit of all three.

I shared with you previously that my marriage was dying, so my thoughts, walk, and relationship with God suffered. How many of us know that what I am saying will not end well? Exactly! God will not have any other gods before him. This is stated precisely in Exodus 20:3(KJV) "Thou shalt have no other gods before me." Not calling my husband or my problems a god, but when I put everything before God. All of my worrying, all of my marital issues, and I tried to handle them myself. God stepped out of the way, and my world came crashing down. My marriage, my finances, my life were all affected.

When we step outside of the will of God, so many things take place. I knew that my crown needed to be adjusted. God was calling me, but I did not answer, so He made me answer. God allowed things to come up against me that made me fall on my face before Him. I had to surrender all to Him. I had to reevaluate myself. It was no longer about saving my marriage, but it was about saving me. It was about saving my soul. I know you are wondering how you adjust your crown. How do you get that relationship with God back once you have lost it?

You may have left God, but He never left you. I thought God left me, but it was me who left Him. Getting back to God is so simple. I had to go back to the beginning. I had to go back to my first love, which is God himself. Nothing else mattered, not my husband, not my children, just me and God. I had to repent and ask for forgiveness. The things that I was experiencing in my marriage were causing spiritual death. So, for me to adjust my crown, my carnal way of thinking had to die. I had to step into my spiritual self. I had to die daily to sin. If I did not kill it, it would kill me and my marriage. I had to read my word daily and pray without ceasing. I prayed for results, and slowly my crown was adjusted. It was like I was a student of life; my soul was the subject, and my God was the teacher. My life and my marriage were at stake. I was learning how to be a godly wife. Adjusting my crown was all about me coming to grips with who I am in Christ and owning it. It was about the power that I possess within me. The power to speak those things that are not as if they are so. The power to pray over my husband's life and demand change. The power to change my destiny. My walk and talk both had to change. My walk had to align with the spiritual walk that God had designed for my life. My crown is worn for God's glory. My crown is my ability to stand with God's power. My crown was God dealing with the issues of my soul. My crown is redemption. My crown, in all its glory, is a representation of who I am in Christ Jesus. I am His daughter. I have royal blood running through my veins. I have been predestined and preordained by God. I am a Queen Built on Sacrificial Suffering; I am the B.O.S.S. Wife.

LESSON 3- ADJUSTING YOUR CROWN

1. I want you to do a self-examination. Does your crown need adjusting? If so stop right now and ask God for forgiveness. Ask God to come into your heart and give you a right spirit.

2. In what areas do you feel that you need God to help you with?

3. Are you guilty of seeking validation from the world? If so, what is about you that made you want to be accepted?

4. Have you been so busy or so focused on your husband's crown that you have forgotten your own? If you have not done this, I want you to repent and return to your first love, which is God.

CHAPTER 4

BEWARE OF THE INFLUENCERS

Guard Your Marriage

If you do not take anything else from this book, I want you to know and understand that God has given you the assignment as a wife to protect and cover your marriage. Your marriage is an honor given to you by God himself, and who you are as a wife should not be taken lightly. Your marriage is valuable, and it must be protected. Because the marriage bond is so sacred, your marriage should be treated like an exquisite hotel VIP membership exclusive for only two people, and that is you and your husband. When both of you stood before God and stated your vows, you two agreed to protect each other. Marriage is about protecting each other's soul and not allowing anyone to break through the barrier and destroy what you have worked so hard to build. It is your spiritual obligation as a wife to guard your marriage in prayer with all your heart. As you guard your marriage, I want you to remember this one important thing BEWARE of the Influencers. Who are the influencers, you ask? The influencer can be your friend, your family, or even your foe. The influencer does not always have to be a person. It could be a job, a thing, or a habit. Either way, you must become the protector of your marriage even when your marriage is going well, and you should always be looking out for the Influencer.

Sometimes it may not be our intention, but the outside influencer somehow always makes their uninvited way into the marriage. They come in surreptitiously meaning, without notice. It is an infiltration to gain access to the marriage. Believe me, when I tell you this, I did not guard my marriage as I should have. I allowed people to come in. There is no need for me to be angry about the entry when I invited them in. I confided in people who had no business knowing what was going on in my home. Take it from me, your girlfriends do not need to know EVERYTHING that goes on between you and your husband. You will thank me for this advice later. Some lessons come easy, and some come hard. I had to learn this the hard way or, better yet, the heart way because my heart always got in the way. Some people will take your kindness for weakness. That is why I am telling you so that you will learn from my mistakes.

All advice is not good advice, so be mindful of who is advising you. Honestly, I was young and gullible. Wanting friends and not realizing who I was. I was too trusting. I opened the box. I opened the door, and I let them in. Here is some food for thought: just because they are family does not mean that they were there for me. I did not even know I was the enemy. I was not aware of the Family Influencers or their feelings. I was too loose with who I entrusted with my marriage business. One thing about the enemy or the devil is that he is very cunning. He did not come in a red suit with horns as he is often portrayed. He came in subtly; he came in through someone that I loved. It could have been a friend, a foe, or a family member. The enemy came, and he came with a vengeance.

I know what it is like to have to fight for your marriage. That is why I am telling you to guard your marriage with all your heart. You have the task of standing in the gap for your marriage and your husband. As you guard your marriage in prayer, you should be praying for protection from the things and people that could tear it apart. You must build a wall of protection around your marriage to keep unwanted intruders out. Be careful of who you let influence your marriage and who you let into your marriage. It is your duty as a wife and your responsibility as the Queen to protect her King, which is your husband and your kingdom, which is your home. Remember, there is no room for any outside guests. So, beware of the Influencers.

Sideline Intruders

Some Influencers (Intruders) are not invited or welcome into the marriage. Their only connection to your marriage would be through an inside informant (FAMILY). Beware of the Sideline Intruders. At first, they may appear to be #TeamMarriage. They appear to be rooting for your team. Warning! BEWARE! These are the ones that come dressed up as if they are the main guest at a masquerade ball. They dress as sheep in wolves' clothing until their true identity is unmasked. When the mask comes off, what is in their hearts is revealed. Be mindful because their participation can be a little deceiving, as they may parade themselves around as if they are your personal cheerleaders, cheering and applauding for the marriage every step of the way, only for you to find out later that they have been the ones cheering against the marriage. Their main objective was to penetrate the protected barrier of the marriage bond.

Warning Beware! These Intruders can be standing right next to you or even on the sideline, literally waiting for the demise or the destruction of the marriage. You will recognize them because these are the ones who will always seem to know the latest breaking news and updates about your marriage. They will be the ones throwing the rocks and hiding their hands. But most definitely, they will be cheering for any negative thing to take place in the marriage. They will find pleasure in hearing your bad news. Beware of the Sideline Intruders.

Mother-Outlaw

When you marry the man; knows and understands that his family does come along with him. As his wife, you should try to get to know his family, especially if the family is important to him. As we talk about the family influencers, one family member sticks out above all the rest. She is probably the closest to him outside of yourself, and she would be the greatest influencer of them all. She is your Mother-In-Law. For those of you who have a great rapport with your Mother-In-Law, consider that as a blessing and cherish her always. But now I am talking to the ones who have had an up-close personal encounter with the influencer that I call the Mother-Outlaw.

Warning! Beware of her influence because it may be damaging to your marriage in years to come. There is an old saying, "Never judge a book by its cover," so in this case, you would want to open it up and read it before giving an opinion. Do the same thing when it comes to your Mother-Outlaw. Do not be quick to judge but always be on the lookout. Be able to discern the spirit that is right in front of you. Looking at her from the exterior, she may seem to be a very loving and caring person. She is one that you would have no problem referring to as "Mom." But her internal picture shows a different person. This Mother-Outlaw may appear to be a walking book of knowledge, and you would agree that she is one that knows everything about how your marriage, her marriage, and everyone else's marriage should operate. In your mind, you view her as an expert. She is a good example of a hardworking woman and mother and not to mention she does give you some good advice from time to time. She has also told you not to take anything off any man, including her son. She would not get into your marriage issues, for she is neutral, and she does not play sides. You put all your trust in her because you were under the impression that she has your best interest at heart. Her advice seems to be wise, genuine, and real from a motherly perspective. What you do not know about the Mother-Outlaw is that she has a hidden agenda and ulterior motive to sabotage and end the marriage by any means necessary. But what you did not know is that she has been having behind-the-scenes conversations concerning you, and, in her eyes, you are just not the bride she would have chosen for her son. I know this is a hard pill to swallow, but this is a reality.

Beware of the Mother-Outlaw's influence, for she suffers from a condition that I call the overbearing, overshadowing, mother syndrome. She has some hidden issues about her son. Maybe at one point, he was the only man she had in her life, and now she will not allow you, his wife, or anybody else to take him from her. Physically we know that the umbilical cord was cut at the time of her son's birth, but for some reason, there is still a connection between the two of them. This is understandable because he is her son.

As a mother, she loves her son dearly. But some love can appear to be overbearing and overshadowing, which would make it impossible for her son to cleave to his wife when he is still attached to his mother in her womb. Because of their connection or attachment, the son may not feel comfortable letting go of their relationship and cleaving to his wife, for the values of his mother's opinion and her approval of his wife means so much. Her acceptance is what he thinks is needed. This type of intrusion can prove to be detrimental to any marriage.

A word of advice to the wife who is having a hard time dealing with the Mother-Outlaw's intrusion, I want to reassure you that God is yet in control of everything. I know that it is not easy, especially when you know that you have gone above and beyond as her daughter-in-law, but do not give up and do not give in. When you married your husband, you married him only. His family just came as a bonus, good or bad. Stop trying to be accepted by them. You must come to grips with the reality that your Mother-Outlaw may NEVER accept or like you. She may have loved his last girlfriend or wife. But it is okay. Guess what? It does not matter because he chose you as his wife. This is one of those moments in your marriage where you will have to stand as a godly wife and let your Mother-Outlaw know that you are not going anywhere.

Despite everything that may come up against you, despite what she has tried to do to you, you must stand and allow the glory of God to shine through you. Keep in mind that every action does not require a reaction from you. Your reaction to her must reflect the love of God. As difficult a task as this may be, you must deal with the Mother-Outlaw how you would want God to deal with you. God gives us His grace and His mercies daily when we do not deserve it, so you should do the same to her. If you find yourself having some resistance in this area, I truly understand because you are human. I have not always been at a place of peace concerning the Mother-Outlaw. Let truth be told, I had some let-go issues involving anger and unforgiveness towards the Mother-Outlaw. It is only when you mature in God that you will understand that vengeance is not yours it is the Lords. I am a testimony that God will fight all your battles.

Friend Influencer

This Influencer is one that is so important to you because she may have been there from the very beginning. She is your ride or die. She is your girl, your best friend. She has even been there before you had the husband, and now that you have the husband, you cannot seem to let go of your friend. Not that you need to, but you should have limitations on how much time you do spend. You want to make sure your time with your friend does not overshadow time with your husband. I want you to beware that spending more time with your friends than with your spouse can cause a disconnect in your marriage. This advice does not only go for the wife but the husband as well. Beware of your Friend Influencer. I get it.

I have girlfriends, so I understand that you sometimes need that girl's day out. To have a peace of mind, you need a moment when you can let your hair down and be your true selves but know that there is a limit and a line that does not need to ever be crossed, or it could be detrimental to the marriage. You must be so in tune with your marriage and know your boundaries. Beware of the single or divorce friend influencer. She may not be tied down, making it easy for her to move and maneuver, but not you. Some of the things you used to do before you got married you cannot do anymore. Partying all the time is not an option. If your friend is not there yet, she might not understand your role as a godly wife.

Beware of the male friend Influencer. We all may have that friend who is closer to us than a brother, which is okay. Some friendships of the opposite sex do require discernment. If that friend cannot be a friend of your husband, then maybe you might need to reevaluate that friendship. Sometimes a male friend can unknowingly be out to sabotage the marriage. Look at the relationship from your husband's view. You may not see this because you are too close to a relationship. Remove your blinders. Yes, you might call him brother, and he might call you sister. Just make sure this friendship is simply platonic. Note if your husband can not be included in a text message or phone call, then that friendship may need to be reconsidered.

Lastly, be mindful of the intimate details that you share with any of your friend's male or female. Your friends do not need to know EVERYTHING that goes on in your marriage. No marriage is perfect, it is not out of the ordinary to have issues. It is how you deal with those issues that make the difference. I know that it is human nature to go to our friends when something pops off or a problem occurs. The problem is that we will run to our friends before we even think about getting on our knees and praying to God for guidance. Some of your friends can not even advise themselves better yet give you advice. Be careful who you let influence your marriage. Beware of the Friend Influencer.

Outside Intruder

This influencer is a little bit tricky because you may not always see her coming. Beware because this one can come in silently with no warning. She goes by the title of Outside Intruder. The Outside Intruder is just that she comes in from the outside. She could very well be his co-worker or an old friend. She is very crafty in her pursuit. She is well aware that he is married, but it intrigues her even more. The friendship may begin as something simply platonic. There is no harm in having friends, right? The interaction between them may start with a passing glance at one another, then maybe a simple hello or goodbye. The casual encounter continues with a mere compliment here and there, but something that was said made your spouse captivated. Could it have been a compliment on his attire or his cologne? This is something that you use to do. Whatever it was, it sparked his curiosity. Then the plot thickens, and the daily conversations have now become their ritual. You being his wife, have no idea what is unfolding right before your eyes. But you noticed something about him. He now pays a little more attention to what he wears to work and how he smells.

You also notice that his once unlocked cell phone now has a passcode added. As you try to wrap your head around things, you know that you two are not having any issues, so you brush it off as your insecurities. Little do you know that this Influencer, or might I say an intruder, has managed to slither in through casual conversation and by exchanging a phone number. She has piqued his curiosity, and what started as casual conversation turned into mutual consenting text messages, and the daily conversations have graduated into nightly communication. As the texting continues, they connect so well as if they were soul mates. She appears to be saying all the right words by just texting to say hello. How is your day going, or did you get something to eat yet. Texting will lead to lunch, and lunch will lead to dinner. Dinner will lead to her bedroom. Now your husband has connected his soul to someone other than you. You may be feeling that everything is wonderful and your marriage is going well. Only to find out later that an unwanted Intruder had entered your sacred space.

Your Influence

This Influence is the greatest of them all. You must beware of Your Influence. It can either be negative or positive. This is done by the mere words that proceed from our lips. We must watch what we say, how we say it, and who we say it to when speaking of our marriage. Sharing a little too much information may become an issue for your marriage. Try not to be so open with your thoughts about your marriage or your husband, for you never know who is listening.

This bit of information is very important about your influence. Do not start anything that you cannot continue, like keeping the house clean, cooking dinner, taking care of your body, keeping your hair done. You know all the things that make us as women look good. With your influence, you want to make him feel that he is important. (If you do not make him feel this way, someone else will.) Note that his appearance might alter, but he expects yours not to (your belly, gut, no makeup, no weave). How you got him is how you want to keep him. Intrigued and Interested in his bride. Do not let yourself or your self-esteem go. We all have busy lives, working the 9 to 5 jobs, taking care of the house, the children, and everybody else, but it is important for you to make time for you and your spouse. Your influence controls marriage.

LESSON 4- BEWARE OF THE INFLUENCER

1. Have there been moments when you allowed negative thoughts and words to control your relationship with your husband?

2. Do you have a good relationship with your husband's family? Specifically, with his mother? If not, have you tried to make things, right? Write down seven things that you would like to change regarding your relationship with your husband's family: especially his mother

3. Have you allowed friends to come into your marriage unannounced? I want you to close your eyes and look at things from your husband's perspective and see if anything is out of line about the friends you have.

4. Reflecting on your marriage issues, have you made it easy for an outside intruder to enter? Do you suspect that an outside intruder has come in? If so, what are your thoughts about this? Do you want your marriage?

5. Have you been guilty of pushing your husband away to an outside influencer? What steps will you take to end this connection? Begin to pray for God to severe this connection in Jesus name.

CHAPTER 5

THE HARDEST HIT EVER

Breaking Point

I believe there will come a time in everyone's life when they will experience what I call a breaking point, an unwanted truth, or maybe just the hardest hit ever experienced. Believe me when I tell you, life has a way of knocking you to your knees. I said to you in the introduction that I would be as transparent as possible with you concerning my marriage, and I meant just that. I told you this would be me raw and uncut. I am here to share my unwanted truth with you. You know life can hit you so hard sometimes that you do not even see it coming. Well, in my case, I should have seen this coming from the very beginning of my marriage, as I reflect on one day, in particular, my wedding day. All the warning signs were there, but I refused to pay attention.

As I sat in the limousine, a teary-eyed young bride watching her bridesmaids from the exterior window. I observed their botched-up dresses' compliments of a not-so-stable seamstress, to my wedding ceremony starting an hour later, to the unwanted guest at the rehearsal dinner the night before all were signs of things to come. Life sort of happens sometimes, or does it? I am a strong believer that nothing just happens but that things do happen for a reason. Things can happen in our lives due to the people, good or bad, that we allow to be a part of our lives. Sometimes God will use those same people for His purpose. If His purpose is to reveal their truth, then He will reveal them to you. The problem is, in life, we think that we want to know the truth. Honestly, we do not want to know the truth at all. Truth be told, some of us cannot handle the truth. That unwanted truth does hurt. It hurts more than you could ever begin to imagine. It can knock you unconscious spiritually, mentally, and even physically. That is what my unwanted, unexpected, and unwelcomed truth did to me.

You've Got Mail

Let me tell you about one of the hardest hits that I ever experienced in my marriage. It was the day that my unwanted truth became my reality. It appeared to me in the form of a message, "You've got mail." Many messages, rumors, phone calls had come before, but not like this one. How many of you know that this is the day that things got really REAL for me? I did not send for this message, neither was I expecting it, but it came. The one place that I thought was safe from intruders. My castle, my home, was my safe zone. When something of this magnitude happens, we think this came from the devil. I remember having a conversation with the devil saying, you could not be coming for me in my own home. Sure enough, the devil did come for me with a vengeance too, I was not prepared, and neither was I ready. My home was supposed to be protected from the stench of this sinful world. How could it be when I had no power. When it comes to the enemy and spiritual warfare, there is no neutral ground. Nothing is off-limits. Although this home invasion took place by the devil, it was allowed by God to reveal and uncover my unwanted truth.

The words You've got mail resonated in my spirit and my soul. Who would have ever thought that my unwanted truth was just a click away? If I just click this button right here, I will get the answer to all my questions. I did what any woman would do. I opened the message, and my heart dropped. To my surprise, it was filled with visuals from a desperate young woman wanting to make her truth relevant. Relevant for her or relevant for me, whatever the intention may have been. She wanted it exposed. She wanted him exposed. She sent the message to get her point across not only to me but to him. Her truth became my reality. The visuals she sent included her man, my HUSBAND.

Remove the Blinders

I do not think anything that we do would prepare us for a time such as this one. Now let us back it up for a moment and be real. There were signs, but I ignored them. I did not pay attention to them. Instead of facing it, I put on blinders. I admit that I had my blocker shades on because I did not want to face the truth. Ladies, that feeling in your gut is real. Listen to it. Pay attention to it. At that very moment, my husband's infidelity was exposed. This was not a one-night stand but an entire relationship. It appears that this relationship took place right under my nose. You might be thinking, boy was he good? Not really. I was just in denial.

When the devil sets a trap, it may be easy to get into but much harder to get out of. My husband was wrapped up in a web of deceit, deception, and denial. I had no other option. I did what any wife would do. I confronted him. There was no denying it. How could he? But he did what any man with everything to lose would do – he denied everything. It did not matter that the pictures, the video, and the text messages contained images of his face, but it was not him in his mind. Instead of facing the truth, which was his truth, he walked away (more like he ran away), and you know what? I let him. As much as I wanted him to admit it, I knew deep in my heart. He would not.

Fresh Start or Not

After separating for a short period, we decided to leave the past behind us and start over. A fresh new start or was it? Well, the devil had a trap set because he knew that my husband still had a weakness, and he wrestled with somethings like his selfish desires. As I was thinking we were on to a fresh new start, that was not my husband's desire in his heart. It was not that he wanted us to start over; he did not want me to start over. I was blindsided. I did not know that the communication with the desperate young woman had continued off and on or on and off, whatever the case may be. It had continued. What I thought had ended was still very much attached.

The next hit, the one that took me out it was vicious. It knocked me so hard that my knees buckled; it was the day that my husband, after 22 years of marriage, confessed not just the relationship, I thought was over but all his infidelity throughout our entire marriage. Maybe he had some kind of weird epiphany? Maybe he was experiencing a midlife crisis, maybe he was prepared to die, or maybe it was just God convicting him in his spirit. Whatever the case may have been, he decided to release this valuable piece of information to me. He laid it out on the table, he did not hold anything in, and he exposed himself and all of his dirt too. I did not want to hear it. But he shared with me anyway the fact that he was tired of carrying this burden around. Once he released it, he felt that a weight had been lifted off of his shoulders, and I felt like a weight dropped directly on mine. Let me tell you something that was the hardest pill I ever had to swallow in my life. Every emotion you can think about having I had. I felt like an absolute fool. I do not care how much you think you would be prepared for something like this, it just does not happen that way. The fresh start was not happening.

Be Careful What You Ask For

I forgot to mention that when I got that gut feeling deep inside, I began to talk to God. I had been praying to God specifically for this very moment. Be careful what you ask God for because He may give it to you. Now, that is exactly what He did for me, and when that moment came, I was not ready to receive it. I had been asking God over and over again to reveal my husband to me. Because something did not feel quite right, He did just that, and I was not ready. My crown was not fitting. As much as I love God, I was not thinking about God when I got that news. Nothing godly was in me. Rage and anger had arrived. This one moment felt like it should have been a forgiving moment, he FINALLY confessed, but it turned into a moment filled with unforgiveness, resentment, hatred, and disappointment. At that very instant, I gave up on my marriage. I threw in the towel, it was over, and I was over it. I knew beyond a shadow of a doubt that I no longer wanted my marriage, so I threw my hands up and said, "You can have this marriage. I am done." I decided I did not want to be his wife anymore. How much hell does one person have to endure? I took off my crown, and I laid it down. I said to myself he was never my king. He was never my husband. All the years I spent being a good wife was for what NOTHING. I was just a mere trophy on the shelf. A prize possession to show off to his friends who did not have one, a good one to be exact.

I Lost My Desire To Love

I could not believe that I spent most of my life believing in a marriage that was a lie from the very beginning. I created this fairy tale marriage the good girl meets the bad guy, and she changes his whole life.

I did not realize that he would change mine forever. I was so hurt that I put up a wall, I shut down, and I shut him out. I had no desire to see him, be with him, or even sleep next to him because, as far as I was concerned, he was not touching me anymore. I was hurting badly, and all I could focus on is the fact that he hurt me. How do you hurt someone that you allegedly love? Yes, it appeared that he was hurting too because he saw me hurting. But I did not know because he was such a good actor. I did not know to believe him or not.

We did not tell our children. We did not tell our family or friends. We were very silent about the state of our marriage. No one knew what we were going through. We still lived in the same house, slept in the same bed, but we were operating as a separate union. Everybody around us thought we were still together; he spent more of his time away from the house because he could not stand to see me cry, and I could not stand to see his face. My crown was tarnished. I lost my desire to love, and I lost my desire for my husband.

I did not go to God about any of this. I took it upon myself to handle this one. How many of you can relate to this? I gave up on my marriage. I honestly felt God gave up on me. I felt God had given up on us. How many of you know those feelings I felt did not come from God? The devil was happy. He was rejoicing! He won! The devil was delighted. He finally accomplished what he set out to do. That was to break me. I became so depressed, but nobody knew. Let me tell you one thing about depression. You can try to conceal it, but it has a funny way of revealing itself. My body exposed the very thing that I tried so hard to hide. Although I thought I could hide my depression under my covers, with my tears and nobody would ever know, my hair said otherwise. I lost my hair where it was very noticeable. I did something drastic and cut it all off. The depression affected my eating habits. I had no desire to eat, so I lost a little weight. It was a hot mess. I had no desire for anything, especially love.

I Do Not Want To Forgive

Instead of forgiving my husband, I constantly reminded him of the pain that he inflicted on me. Every day for about a month, I reminded him of the hardest hit ever. I gave 100% to a man that only gave me maybe 50%, and to hear him say he almost threw it all away for 10% that did something to me in my soul. My crown was not fitting, neither did I want to adjust it. The Boss Wife in me was broken. I had no desire to pick up my Bible or any Bible; pick it up for what? I had become angry and bitter. Love and kindness were not in me. I was rebellious and stubborn. My anointing was stifled.

The devil sent a direct hit to my location, and he used weapons more powerful than me. He has no power but at this time, neither did I. This hit was supposed to take me out. One thing about the enemy he knows when you are not in your word. He does not come when you are strong. He strategically plots and plans. He comes when you are most vulnerable. He comes to rob, steal, and destroy but remember he cannot come without God's permission.

God has a purpose attached to my destiny, so the enemy's plan did not work. It was not through my prayers this time that our marriage was saved. I stopped praying for the marriage. It was through the prayers of my husband. He laid on his face before God, begging and pleading for God to save his marriage. He asked God not to take me away from him. See, I had completely given up, and it was over. I meant just that. I just did not know how I was going to leave. I knew that I was existing. I had a foolproof exit plan in my mind, and I was going to use it. Forgiveness was not an option for me.

Our Plans Are Not God's Plans

Remember this one thing our plans are not God's plans. God did not tell me to move. As much as I hated my husband, God did not tell me to move. But I was going to. It was not until God convicted me in my spirit and said to me, "You asked me for this. You asked me to convict him in his spirit to where he will have no other recourse but to tell you the truth about everything. You asked for this. I gave you the truth. But now you turn around and crucify him for telling you the truth. Have you not crucified him enough? He is my child too. What are you saying to him when he asked you for forgiveness, and you say you do forgive, but, in your heart, you do not? You are constantly reminding him of his sin. Enough! This is bigger than you, and this is not about you. This is about my purpose and my plan for your marriage. This is about his soul. You will not move. Your test will be a testimony for all wives that there is hope."

I know I was hearing God, but at that moment, I was operating in the flesh. I did not want to hear that. I could not begin to see what God had in store for us. I could not believe it. I did not want to believe it, and I was too stubborn to see it. I just wanted to focus on my pain alone and my feelings. I asked God, "Did you not see what he did to me," and God said, "I did, but again it is not about you. It never was. It was about my kingdom. It is all for my Glory. Your marriage has been the sacrifice. You will survive this infidelity. Where people thought your marriage had died, I will revive it, and your marriage will be saved. You two will be my TESTIMONY! I will get the glory."

LESSON 5- THE HARDEST HIT

1. Have you ever experienced unbearable pain from a breakup? If so, what kind of pain? How did you handle this pain? Did you ask God to help you? To heal you?
2. Have you experienced infidelity? How did this make you feel? Have you been healed from this pain?
3. After reading this chapter, do you think that you would be able to forgive infidelity? Are you wrestling with unforgiveness?
4. If you experienced infidelity in your marriage, write a letter to your spouse and tell them exactly how you feel. How did you feel after you wrote the letter? Now ask God to help you forgive so that you can move forward with your life.

CHAPTER 6

LORD, I NEED A HEART TRANSPLANT!

What Would You Do

I know most women reading this would think that they would know exactly what to do if they ever discovered their husband's infidelity. I know I did. I am sure you are sitting there right now, playing the scene in your head repeatedly as if you were a movie on how you would react and what you would do. But wait! What I want you to understand is that there is a different view when you are on the outside looking in. My question to you is, how would you handle that pain? Would you respond in rage and anger, or would you become emotional and clingy? I do not care where you are in your life on the top or the bottom, having money or not having money; believe me, no one is exempt from experiencing pain. Just because you vow not to fold does not make the next person the weaker being. Everyone handles pain differently when it is presented to them. If you have not experienced it, keep living.

What Did I Do To Deserve This

Sometimes pain can hit us so hard that it touches the inner core of our being. The pain from Infidelity is like no other pain. It can have you questioning what you did to deserve its arrival. This pain is brutal. It has been known to conquer the strongest of men. This kind of pain that I am referring to reaches into the soul. The soul, which is the seat bed of our emotions, houses our feelings, pain, fear, anger, and even our love. This pain runs deep through it. I honestly do not believe there is anything in this life that can prepare you for this kind of pain. I would be lying to you and myself if I told you that I was ready for this type of warfare. As much as I would like to say to you that I had it all together, and I was clothed in the full armor of God, I was not. Neither was I reading and studying my word regularly. I had no weapons of warfare to fight with. Do not get me wrong, I attempted to read my bible, but things got too heavy for me to handle, and I allowed my pain to consume me. I admit that I was not prepared.

After the big reveal of my husband's infidelity surfaced, I experienced all sorts of emotional trauma. I was hurting inside. I was angry, but most of all, I was just tired. The infidelity situation, my marriage, and the man I used to call my husband had sucked the life right out of me; it felt as if I was hit by the biggest boulder ever in my chest. The impact was so heavy that it nearly took my breath away. My heart was heavy, and it could not take it anymore. I do not know why we do this. Maybe it is just our human nature, but I constantly questioned myself, asking what did I do to deserve this? As much as I believed in God, I could not believe that He allowed all these things to happen openly to me within my marriage. I guess it is okay when we experience things in private, and nobody knows. But when our dirty laundry hits the air, boy, it can stink.

Mission Accomplished

When the devil has an assignment to destroy you, I promise you he does not play fair. When he knows that there is a purpose attached to you, he will not stop until his mission is accomplished, or so he thinks it is accomplished. He strategically prepares for his battle against you (his opponent). He studies you, and he knows your every weakness. The devil knew that my marriage and my family meant so much to me. He knew my weakness. So, what did he do? He exposed my weakness to the world. We all have weaknesses. We all wrestle with something. Rather it is an addiction, an emotion, or excessive behavior. We wrestle.

The devil knew exposing my marital issues to the world would send me into a low, gloomy state. Depression was something that I often wrestled with from time to time, and the devil knew it. I call it my shutting down period. My regrouping, resetting period. I can call it what I want to call it, but it was depression. If you have ever experienced depression, then you can relate to where I am coming from. I was hit so hard with depression that I did not want to get out of bed. I laid lifelessly in the bed for days beside the fact that I would get up, shower, and go to work; I was not moving.

The enemy had me thinking that God had forgotten about me, and I was all alone. I was in a comatose state with no desire to do anything. In a matter of weeks, I lost my hair. I woke up one morning with my hair on my pillow. Believe me. Depression can do something to the body. I looked as if I had been recently diagnosed with some disease derived from all the internal pain I was carrying. That included all the bottled-up emotions that I held in, like the anger, frustration, hurt, abandonment, rejection, and all the tears I had been crying for years. The devil's mission was accomplished. He finally got me to my lowest point. How many of you know that it ain't over until God says it is over?

God Had A Plan, But He Forgot To Tell Me

Despite what it may look like to the natural eye and the world, God always had a plan. But I guess He forgot to let me in on the secret. Maybe if He had done so, I would have been a little more prepared for the pain. The pain I was experiencing had caused some spiritual, emotional trauma, and let me tell you. It was like God Himself dispatched His angels to come and save me. I was admitted to the spiritual trauma unit and in need of God (the heavenly surgeon) to give me a heart transplant. Looking through my spiritual lenses, I could only imagine seeing the angels rolling me into the Trauma unit, prepping me for spiritual surgery. My heart required a transplant. There was only one surgeon that was on call this day, and that was God. The Lord needed to rescue me. Spiritually I needed to be resuscitated. This situation had become way too much for me to handle.

Have you ever forgotten how to pray? I did. I had gotten so into my feelings of everything going on around me that I forgot how to pray or even pick up my word. Honestly, I did not want to pick up my word. Sometimes you just get tired of being tired. But when God has a purpose for you, and it is attached to your marriage, you cannot dictate to Him what or how you want to go through your test. You must go through it. God showed me that I was not in charge; He was. God performed a rescue and a recovery on me because He knew that my heart had become bitter. Oh yes, I held on to anger, hatred, stubbornness, and revenge. All I knew is that I did not forgive my husband, and I wanted him to feel the same pain that I felt. In my heart, I wanted revenge. I was not thinking about praying for my husband or our marriage. God had a plan, but He forgot to tell me that in my going through, He was going to use my husband to help save me. What I did not know is that behind the scenes, my husband had been praying for me. He had asked God to deliver me. He begged God not to take me from him. My healing did not happen immediately, but something did change in me.

My Confession

Change does not come instantaneously. It does take time. Sometimes it takes a lifetime. Change is a process with a purpose attached to it. Change did not happen for me right away. It was not until I had a heart-to-heart conversation with God and openly confessed to Him what I had been feeling. I cried out to Him, I repented, and He heard me. At that very instant, I do believe that God delivered me. God not only rescued me, but He also recovered me. He did a mouth-to-mouth resuscitation on me with His Holy Spirit. God breathed life into my much-needed spirit, man. Not only did God breathe on my spirit, but He also breathed on my marriage. When I confessed to God my pain, He restored me. God restored some of the areas that I thought were dead. I honestly thought my marriage was over. The change and healing did not magically happen for us overnight, but in the process, God gave me a new love for my husband. God restored our marriage. The marriage that I thought was dead, the marriage that I gave up on, God began to rebuild it. He rebuilt the trust that was missing.

How many of you know that God had a lesson for me in all of this? God wanted to teach me something. Despite how ugly the sin may have been, God recovered us from it. While I focused on my husband's sin, God wanted me to look at my husband through His eyes. He wanted me to see that just as I come to Him in sin, I am not perfect, and when I ask for forgiveness, He gives me His grace and His mercy. He forgives me. God gave me the same grace; I should have given it to my husband when he asked me for it. But I did not. I held on to my selfish emotions, anger, and bitterness. So, what did God do? Of course, God convicted me in my spirit. He allowed me to see that the way I behaved was not right and pleasing in His eyes. God reminded me that we all fall short of the glory of God. There is no little sin or big sin, sin is just sin in God's eyes, and no one is exempt from sin. No one can cast a stone because no one is perfect. We all fall short of His glory.

God also showed me that I was a hypocrite, I talked about being a Christian, but I was not living like one. I talked about forgiveness. I even forgave others, but I did not forgive my husband. Forgiveness is hard. I will not lie to you. To forgive someone for wrongdoing when you know that you have treated them right is extremely hard to do. But it is required by God. That is all a part of growing in God gracefully. I will be honest. My actions did not reflect the God in me. I was not looking like Christ. I was not behaving like him either. My confession was needed so that My spirit could have a fresh anointing.

On The Road To Recovery

On the road to recovery, both me and my husband had to work hard at rebuilding our marriage. I admit to you that it was not easy for either of us. Our rebuilding process required a lot of patience, a quality that neither of us had when dealing with our marriage or each other. Again, recovery, just like change, is a process for the purpose. There were moments my husband had to endure all my going back and forth, reminding him of his offense. He had to undergo the interrogation period, where I just had to know why. Even though his why did not make sense to me. I wanted to know what caused him to do what he did. What about me made him do it. These were unanswered questions, and I just had to know. To top it all off, he had to deal with the rejection in the bedroom as I had no desire to fulfill my sexual duty as his wife. He had to bear witness to all the tears I cried and still offer me his love. I would have those moments of insecurity where my husband constantly reminded me that he was truly sorry for ever hurting me and that he knows now how precious I am to him. Not that those words meant anything, but, in the end, they meant everything. My husband was a big part of my recovery. In our communication, God slowly began to restore what was torn down. For us to get to the core of our pain, we had to communicate our feelings. This was, in fact, an area that needed restoration. God allowed us to start communicating without being argumentative. We listened to each other without judging. On this road to recovery, we found out that we both had some underlined issues that had caused problems for us in our marriage.

But God always had a plan. God gave us a fresh new love for each other. If God can do it for us, and I know we were in bad shape, then God can do it for anybody. Recovery, Restoration, and Revitalization of the marriage can only be achieved by including God.

Handling Turbulence

If you are experiencing any turbulence in your marriage, do not give up. I know that it can be hard. Anything worth keeping is worth fighting for. The easiest thing in the world that you could ever do is give up and guess what happens, the devil wins. He gets the victory. When God should have been the one receiving the glory. You allowed the devil to win. Just think about how many marriages have ended prematurely, and God did not tell them to end. God wanted their marriage to be a blessing and a testimony of what He could do. But they allowed their emotions to take control of the situation instead of waiting on God.

As much as I wanted to move and leave my husband, God said no. Believe me. It was not in my strength that I stayed. It was God that kept me in my marriage. I had enough. I was done. My marriage was over. But my plan was not God's plan. God knew we would experience turbulence. God knew my thoughts and feelings. God rescued and recovered me for a time such as this. He knew that I would be writing this book and that I would be telling my story to the world. God knew that my story needed to be heard and that I would not be afraid to put all my business in the street and expose it. God let me know that what was once dead, He would give it life, and that is what He did. He has given us a new marriage and another opportunity to get it right finally. Do not get me wrong, we do still have our bad days. Because we are works in progress. We are nowhere near being perfect, but we are better than we were. We love each other so much more. We desire nothing but to see other couples who are going through similar turbulent situations be able to overcome and restore the marriage bond. We get it. The marriage is under attack because the devil is mad about the union. It is our duty and responsibility to be a guide to help other couples get through it.

I Did Not Think We Would Get To This Point

Believe me, we did not think that we would be together today. I honestly did not think we would get to this point. But God did. A point of restoration for us? After all, God has shown us and after all we have been through, we still believe that there is hope even after experiencing infidelity, hurt, rejection, and pain. We know God can recover any dead situation. Look at us. He recovered, restored, and revived our marriage. We are stronger, and we are wiser. God can breathe the breath of life on that very thing (your marriage) that everyone has counted out and said was dead. God can get the Glory.

The devil targeted our marriage. He set every trap possible, and in some instances, you witnessed it; he succeeded. Here is the catch. God allowed him because God knew that it was bigger than any trap the devil could ever set; it was God's ordained plan. God's plan is perfect. No matter how much I can question the beginning of it all. No matter how I could question the process I had to go through, God still had a plan no matter how many regrets I had. God knew that the day would come when He would have to rescue me. I have helped so many, but now it was time for God to help me. God knew that I would be so hurt that He would have to cover me with His feathers. God knew that I would be so weak that His angels would have to lift me up. God knew that I would surrender all to Him, and He would restore me and my marriage. God knew from the beginning because He predestined and preordained my life. God knew how He would use our marriage as a sacrifice. And through all the filth, dirt, and grimy behavior, God worked on the heart of my husband. God brought restoration to our marriage so that we can be a blessing. It took for me to go through the trauma unit to have my heart recovered, restored, and revived so that I could be a testimony for you.

LESSON 6- I NEED A HEART TRANSPLANT

1 Do you feel that you struggle with unforgiveness? Did this unforgiveness come from a traumatic experience in a past relationship or your marriage? Have you been able to deal with this?

2. Do you need a heart transplant?

3. Are you on the road to recovery in your marriage? If not, what areas would you like to see restored?

4. Have you experienced some turbulence in your marriage? I want you to write out a list of things that you want to see change in your marriage—for example, Communication, Romance, Intimacy, etc.

CHAPTER 7

BECOMING THE BOSS WIFE – WHAT A JOURNEY

W_{hy Me?}

I honestly believe that we all have a call upon our lives. The word of God says that many are called, but few are chosen. I believe God chose me to be an example for you. Not every woman is built for this process. The entire time writing this book, I contemplated back and forth, often questioning God as to the reasoning behind birthing this book. I felt that I was not worthy of delivering to you something of this caliber. I knew that God had an assignment of great magnitude, but I was unsure why He would have chosen me to complete it. Not downplaying who I am. I know whose I am and who I am. It was more about what God wanted me to say and how it would be presented to you. God put this story in me to bring it to life and for it to be a testimony. So, of course, I was a little overprotective of how it would be perceived, and I delayed its birth. It is true that "Becoming the Boss Wife" is a book, but it is also my baby. Just as a mother is protective of her baby, so was I of my book. I was protective of the impact that it would have on the world. I needed to have a clear understanding from God of what it is really about my life, my story, and my journey that would be so compelling that it would change your life and the lives of other wives and women. Truthfully if it were up to me, this book would not have been written. But God told me to "Write the book."

The Boss Wife

Genesis 2:18 (KJV) states, "And the Lord God said, it is not good that the man should be alone; I will make him a help meet for him." From the very beginning, God knew that your husband needed you. A Boss Wife. A helpmate. It is astounding to me how God purposefully formed the woman. The woman's existence was so important to God that He administered a surgical procedure to bring her to life. Yes! God was the first surgeon. If we were to look at Genesis 2:21 (KJV), we would see evidence of this. It states clearly, "And the Lord God caused a deep sleep to fall upon Adam and he slept; and he took out one of his ribs and closed up the flesh instead thereof." Sounds familiar? Sounds a lot like surgery to me. God performed the very first operation on man for you. Genesis 2:22(KJV) states, "And the rib, which the Lord God had taken from man, made he a woman and brought her unto the man." When God created you, He created a perfect thing, not perfect in the sense of having no flaws, but He designed you with perfection and a purpose

Becoming The Boss Wife has always been about you, the wife. You were indeed created to complete your husband. But it is more important that you do understand who you really are. As the Boss Wife, you are the modern-day Proverbs 31 woman. A virtuous woman, a woman of great character, and one who cannot be set at a price. There is no value high enough to determine your worth. You know your worth. If you do not know your worth, then it is time that you do. It is time for you to value yourself. Value yourself more than anything else. It is time for you to appreciate yourself. You are beautiful and uniquely made by God. You are confident in the you that God created. As a woman who has gone through the fire, I understand that we can occasionally lose our confidence because of this thing called life. Sometimes our lives can get so hay wired that we could get lost in our mess, and we lose our God-given identity. Listen to me: do not forfeit your soul for loving a man way too much.

As the Boss Wife, your relationship with God means everything. This is a necessary attribute for you to be one with God. It trumps any other relationships. God loves you so much that He designed you uniquely. You are not a knockoff. You are authentic, and you cannot be copied. When God made you, nothing about you can be duplicated. God poured His attributes into you. He gave you intellectual abilities to pursue something, and you obtain. He made you wise with wisdom so that you can be competent and diligent. That is being a Boss. God knew your husband would need for you to have substance, and you bring something to the table. You are an asset, not a liability. Your very existence compliments your husband's swag and his fly. You are the icing on his cake. You are the BOSS WIFE.

My Boss Wife Journey

My Boss Wife journey has been about survival from the very beginning. Marriage is about survival. Only the strong will survive. This is not to scare you, but marriage is not for everybody. Take into consideration all things before attempting this journey. This is a journey that you must be ready for, and I mean really ready for. The Boss Wife journey can be one heck of a roller coast ride. Buckle up and be prepared because marriage comes with highs and lows. When I first got married, I did not have a manual or the skills to succeed in my marriage. I just had to survive. There was a moment in my life when I felt as if I had been handpicked for an episode of the survivor. I had no tools, I had no essentials, I had no bags, and I had no instructions. I had to wing it. This marriage journey left me with bumps and bruises, and I have the emotional scars to prove it. This was one journey that I was not prepared to take as a woman or a wife. Marriage will make you, or it will break you. Be prepared.

My Boss Wife journey was a personal, intimate journey into my life and my marriage. I was tested in every area of my life, especially when it came to my spirituality. When God has a purpose for your life, you have no other recourse but to comply. God said I had to write this book. It did not matter how much I resisted. Guess what? I had to write the book so that God could get the glory. This book is not about me; it was written for you. If I had to do this again, I would do whatever it takes to help save you.

I Could Not See What God Was Doing

Throughout this journey, I could not see what God was doing, but God was preparing me. He was preparing me for you. God knew that one day I would not be afraid. I would face all my insecurities and my fear. FEAR would be out the window, I would shame the devil, and I would speak openly and be transparent about my hurt and pain. The pain in my marriage. Pain that was caused by someone that I deeply loved. I did not know at the time, but I was becoming a Boss Wife. Built on Sacrificial Suffering. I took the L, the loss, so that you, the wife, could live. My marriage was a sacrifice.

I have taken the test to be a Testimony. My testimony is that there is hope for your marriage. Sure, it may look like it is dying right now, but if you really and truly want your marriage, you must step up and take your God-given authority. You must stand with God for your marriage. Step into who you are and own it. You have the power to speak those things that are not if they are so. Know that your marriage is not dead; it only appears that way. You must speak life. You must constantly speak life into your husband's life until it manifest. God has given you that power and authority to do so.

The Marriage Is Being Attacked

Listen to me. I know that the marriage bond is being attacked in such a way that it appears there is no comeback. This is only a smokescreen put up by the devil. He is placing a spirit of fear in us about the marriage. He does not want the marriage to exist. He does not want your marriage to exist. He will do anything within his power to bring about division and separation. He is the head infiltrator. He comes to break all barriers surrounding the marriage. He comes in to rob, steal, and destroy the marriage bond. His ultimate goal is to see that you completely throw in the towel, give up and give in. It is your assignment as a Boss Wife to take your authority back. You better not just lay there and die. There is yet work to do. Girl, get up and fight! This is what I had to do. This is what you are going to do—no more pity party. God would not allow you to do anything else. There is no other recourse but for you to fight for your marriage. Like the Queen on the chessboard, you must fight to protect your King.

I will admit to you that my Boss Wife journey was not easy at all. It was constantly under attack. I had to disconnect my feelings, I had to lace up my boots, and I had to fight for my marriage. Not so much as a physical fight, but a spiritual battle was before me. Only through the grace of God did I survive. It was all a process, and God wanted me to trust Him fully. As much as I wanted to believe that God was with me on this journey, I had my doubts. That was because my crown needed adjusting. I had been so caught up in changing my spouse that I had forgotten about my spiritual walk. If I had been concentrating on my crown and my walk, maybe I could have spotted the influencers' infiltration from afar and not invite them in so willingly. As much as we hate to admit, some of our wounds are self-inflicted.

No Marriage Is Perfect

What I have learned most on this Boss Wife journey is that no marriage is perfect. I do not care how you dress it up, wrap it up or package it. If it is not right, eventually, the stench from the garbage that you are shoveling will be exposed. My marriage was not perfect. My husband was not ready to be a husband, and I was in denial. I thought I could fix him. I tried and tried to fix his crown, only to fail. I think that crowning my husband would have come faster if only I had stepped out of the equation and allowed God to do what He eventually did. Fix my husband's crown. Take it from me. Everyone has problems. Despite what they may want the world to believe, everybody has issues. Every marriage has its problems, some big and some small no marriage is perfect. If you want a successful godly marriage, you must put God first. There is no way around this. There will come a time when you will have to reach out your hand to God and ask for help. I would rather go into battle, knowing that I am not fighting alone than fighting without God. I gave my marriage to God. Simply put, my marriage is about God's business. It is a serious business.

God Is The Headliner

Before I go, I want to leave you with a few golden nuggets. Make sure that you allow God to always be the headliner in your marriage. This is a non-negotiable deal. Only through His leading and guiding will your marriage make it. Filling the Boss Wife's stilettos is a hard-daunting task, so be prepared spiritually for the journey. You must equip yourself with godly instruction daily, which is the Word of God; this will direct your path. When traveling on this journey, remember that you have to travel this road alone, no friends allowed, only you and the Holy Spirit. This is where you will gain your strength. You will have moments when you will have to fast and pray for marriage and your husband. You are a prayer warrior.

God is calling you to step into your position. We already know that The Boss Wife Journey will not be for everybody as the road may get a little rough. Some of you may break a heel along the way. Some may trip and fall on the stumbling blocks of life, and some of you may flat out lose your shoe in the gravel trying to get out of your mess. This journey is a journey for the mature one. A woman or wife with a godly walk. A woman that has a strong desire to see her marriage change. She has no limits because she has faith as a mustard seed. She will speak to the mountain of adversity in her marriage to be moved because God called her to do so. She is a Boss. Built on Sacrificial Suffering. She is the Boss Wife.

This Boss Wife Journey has always had one objective attached to it: to build God's kingdom. Winning souls. Saving dying marriages. Restoring and rebuilding the marriage bond. If you feel that your marriage is on the verge of ending and you have tried everything humanely possible, try God! Try consulting God first concerning your marriage. Do not make hasty decisions. Do not operate in the ways of the world; try God's way. I just want to say to you that there is hope. It may not seem possible. It may even look that way right now. God can heal your marriage. God is the only one that saves your marriage. God can bring restoration to your marriage. God can take away all your pain. View your marriage as God sees it as a testimony. Your marriage has a purpose. What you have gone through has not been in vain your marriage may be attached to someone else's healing. By all means, consult God first and be sure that the man attached to you has a destiny with you. Do not miss out on this opportunity to be used by God. If God confirms to you that your marriage is worth saving, then you have no other choice but to stand up, put on your stilettos, pick up your sword, and fight for your marriage. Remember the Queen must always protect her kingdom and her king.

LESSON 7- BECOMING THE BOSS WIFE

1. Do you love your marriage and your spouse more than God and yourself?

2. How often have you asked the question why you? Why did God allow things to take place in your marriage, hurtful unforgiving things?

3. Do you know that you have purpose? Do you know and understand who you are in God? If the answer to this question is no stop right here put down your pen and ask God what to reveal to you your destiny, your walk, your purpose in life.

4. Do you know that God values you and that He predestined your life to do GREAT things. Think about somethings that you would like to accomplish for yourself and in your marriage and write those things down. Read it 7 times daily until it is manifested in the natural.